Journey
from the
SWAMP

Journey
from the
SWAMP

How to Defeat Shame
& Rediscover Purpose

Valeria Hughes

Journey from the Swamp:
How to Defeat Shame and Recover Purpose

Copyright © 2023 by Valeria L. Hughes

ISBN 979-8-9892898-0-6

Dedication

This book is dedicated to my dear friend, Jamie Leigh Albritton, and my mighty mentor, Marilyn Chennault.

Jamie, you were a treasure but didn't know. You had a great purpose but didn't realize. I deeply miss you, your great insight, your laugh, and your knowledge of all things spiritual. We lost you too soon. Through you, I learned so many things, some of them painful. I was walking this road of healing when we met in the spring of 2009. You brought me into your home in Loveland to care for me when I was too sick to care for myself. You loved fiercely and you lived bravely. May your memory never dim.

Sister Chennault, you were the greatest influence on my early life in ministry. Without you, I surely would have been lost. You inserted yourself into my life on a Friday evening at an Oklahoma youth camp as I sat alone outside the main tabernacle. I was supposed to be on security duty, but God had other plans that night. You showed up and barged right into my inner world, and for that, I will ever be grateful. *What in the world will we do without you?* I asked silently as I stood at your bedside on your last day on earth. Somehow, we've managed to make it this far with the lessons you taught us. Someday soon, we will see you again on the other side.

Special Thanks

Scores of people have asked me for years to write a book. If you are one of those people, thank you. Your insistence has finally paid off! Please buy these books by the case, and gift them to everyone you know since this is all your fault. Blame shift!

To my amazing husband, Rick Hughes, who has been my number one supporter and encourager for this book. Thank you for the many iced coffee runs, the dark chocolate, the wireless keyboard, the insistence that we take a few days to hole up in a wonderful space so I could concentrate on finishing this, and countless other "necessary" items you made sure I had to be successful for this book. My gratitude knows no bounds. You are my better half!

To my son, Blake, and daughter in love, Emily, you are examples of strength as I watch you both live out loud for God and hustle your way to a wonderful life. I am proud of each of you for your devotion to family and strong work ethic.

To my mom, who is a constant pillar of strength and an endless source of "you got this, and pull yourself up" in everything. Mom, don't you know that Dad would be so proud of this book! His buttons would be popping off his shirt.

To my amazingly resilient siblings, VeAna and Dale, love you always. You will always be my li'l sis and li'l bro! To the moon and back, or maybe just to Roy's Chicken and back.

To my Harger family, may you all find the strength to stand strong once again. We are strong only through God.

To my aunt Wanda, who tried to tell me about living strong and being my own person although I somehow didn't get it then. I recall fondly every trip you took me on. Thank you for financing the trip to Singapore that changed my life trajectory!

To my Nonfiction Tribe, you have quite literally pulled this book out of me. I never intended to write this story, but every one of you insisted. Kendra, your book is next! Melani, the permanent boss of NonFiction, you are the greatest cheerleader and crusader I know!

To my devoted friends, Randa and Bethany. What wonderful friends you are always, supporting me through the dark days and questioning my sanity when necessary. Bethany, you are the best and most amazing editor ever! You are my writing sister who completes me and makes me so much better.

To my Wednesday Warrior Zoom friend group, each of you has such a special place in my heart! Thanks doesn't seem adequate since you always know how to clarify my muddy messes and to help me make sense of this crazy world. Someday soon, let's celebrate big in person together somewhere!

To every person from Ponca City who shared my life for thirty years, I owe you more than I can repay. Walking beside you, I had to learn these concepts the hard way. May you ever serve the Lord and reach for your kingdom purpose.

To each Hyphen and OKNextGen and to every person and precious elder in the Oklahoma District, I am indebted to you for a lifetime of learning and service. We are better together. I will not soon forget all our times together at camps, conventions, conferences, and rallies. I charge you to ignite your kingdom purpose in a great flame of Holy Ghost fire across this state. May we work together to haul in the greatest harvest that Oklahoma has ever seen!

Contents

Introduction

saiah 61 illustrates the compelling reason behind this book.

> *The Spirit of the Lord GOD is upon me,*
> *Because the LORD has anointed me*
> *To bring good news to the afflicted;*
> *He has sent me to bind up the brokenhearted,*
> *To proclaim liberty to captives*
> *And freedom to prisoners;*
> *To proclaim the favorable year of the LORD*
> *And the day of vengeance of our God;*
> *To comfort all who mourn,*
> *To grant those who mourn in Zion,*
> *Giving them a garland instead of ashes,*
> *The oil of gladness instead of mourning,*
> *The mantle of praise instead of a spirit of fainting.*
> *So they will be called oaks of righteousness,*
> *The planting of the LORD, that He may be glorified.*
> *Then they will rebuild the ancient ruins,*
> *They will raise up the former devastations;*
> *And they will repair the ruined cities,*
> *The desolations of many generations*
> (Isaiah 61:1-4, NASB).

This, the book I never wanted to write, is my story: open, honest, transparent, and vulnerable. I want to explain a few things about my thoughts before we get started.

9

I would love for people everywhere to be seen and heard concerning what they have thought for most or all of a lifetime is wrong with them. Despite what you think, you are not hopelessly flawed.

I would love for readers to realize that the Word of God has all the answers to their brokenness and the lies they have believed for ever so long.

I wish for readers to have the ability to combat feelings of inadequacy through an understanding of shame.

I wish for readers to find their identity in God and His Word.

I wish for readers to conquer their lack of self-worth, which has held them back, and through Scripture and scriptural principles to move forward with their life purpose and kingdom giftings.

I wish for readers to be free from shame and from the perceptions of failure, personal insufficiency, and inability to accomplish their kingdom purpose.

I wish for readers to step beyond the paralyzing quandary of the swamp of shame and to begin the experience of a life filled with joy, connection, gratitude, and contentment.

I wish for readers to take the major steps outlined in this book that will enable them to find the strength to escape the clutches of the enemy's tactics, to leave the pathways their minds have created from years of overused toxic thought patterns, and, finally, to create pathways that come from mantras, Scriptures, and newly formed neurons.

I wish for readers to allow their guards to go down and their walls of distrust and unbelief to fall.

I wish for readers to exchange the lies they have believed with ammunition against the adversary of their souls through principles that come only by a revelation of who we are in Christ.

Most of all, may God's Spirit use my writing contained here to redeem those years I spent in darkness and misery. If one person is helped, the will of God has been done. Amen.

Bishop Chester Wright has written an amazing deep dive into the scriptural basis of shame. Please, I beg of you! Stop reading now, and buy this resource on the website: *Antioch, the Apostolic Church*. You can find his teaching on the subject from seminars in 2010 and 2011 on a website entitled *Apostolic Iron* (https://www.apostoliciron.com/) and also videos titled *Inner Healing* by Chester Wright on YouTube. The printed resource is an absolute treasure of theological insight, where I found many nuggets of scriptural wisdom on the topic of shame. Please purchase the pdf, *Shame Syllabus*, from his church so you will have the scriptural viewpoint for shame as well. The church at large owes a huge debt of gratitude to Rev. Wright for his endless work and intense study into this almost hidden from view topic.

────────────────────────

This volume emerged from the NonFiction conference in Terre Haute, Indiana, in 2022. Melani Shock and I had many conversations about shame and its debilitating effects on the church. Melani asked me to share my journey from shame, and after I addressed the gathering, an overwhelming number of queries flooded the question-and-answer period. I could not possibly answer every question, and my spirit felt bereft as we closed that session with numerous unanswered questions. My prayer is that this book will answer the complex questions many participants raised that day.

────────────────────────

The Lord transmitted the following early on the morning of the inaugural NonFiction. On November 13, 2021, as I huddled near my bed under a pile of blankets, God spoke through my pen to each precious lady who gathered at that conference and all subsequent events:

> I will meet with you there. I will show you great things. You aren't accustomed to hearing My voice in a way through which I will speak, but know it is My voice. I have always spoken in a still small voice.
> The ladies are tired and some are through. They are not working in My strength and they must learn of Me, for the

next section of the road will be long and hard. The only way to learn of Me is through trials and tests, for it's then I show My power. My Word is given to you as a guide.

Realize that I am trying to teach you to walk with Me and to lean on Me. I never do anything to hurt you. Everything is ultimately for your good. You must be strong in spirit and in mind/heart, for out of these flows your life.

I am always with you in your darkest hour.

Trust Me. Learn of Me. I have many souls to reach with My saving name.

I am strong when you are weary. Learn to come to Me for strength. Sit at My feet, in My presence. It's there you find joy and peace. Through My love, you are complete.

Lean.

Rest.

Learn.

Stay put.

Listen.

These words were kept exactly as I received them from the Lord.

The Revelation

*D*on't let the people who haven't built anything significant tell you how to build the dream God gave you. God's vision for your life won't align with their opinions. Do it anyway."
—Michael Scobey

Swamp. That word conjures all sorts of craziness in my mind. But my imagination has been known to run quite wild at times—usually, at all the wrong times.

Oxford Language Dictionary defines *swamp* as "an area of low-lying ground where water collects as in a bog, marsh, quagmire, or morass." The verb form of *swamp* means "to overwhelm with water or flood." Most interesting, Merriam-Webster states that a swamp is a difficult or troublesome situation. This supplies the most concise definition for this book because that's exactly what shame is: a difficult situation in which most of us find ourselves trapped.

Be prepared to be inundated with floodwaters of healing as you read. You will begin a process to escape the swamp—or that wonderfully awful word, quagmire—where you've been trapped for quite a while. It might come as somewhat of a relief to realize that you're not alone nor ever have been.

═══════════════════

Everything This Book Isn't

Welcome to hope and change! First, let's talk about all the stuff this book is not.

This book is not counseling.

This book is not medical advice.

This book is not "hope it gets better. . . ."

This book is not another story of comparison to the narrative you just told.

This book was written with the goal of coming alongside you so you may realize there is hope for a better day and hope for a better way to live and to process tasks.

This book was borne out of my many weary, exhausting years of struggle. I do not care to have your pity or your sympathy. Life happens to all of us. I simply believe that my previous ordeals will be redeemed when people find healing through the words in this book all because the Lord has ordained this project.

I will be quite open, raw, and vulnerable. Please accept that as my sincere gift to you as you read.

I have found that healing comes when we are open and honest with each other. We belong together. We tell our stories of struggle in a safe community so we can say, "You, too?"

In *Soul Care*, Rob Reimer provides an introductory statement that pertains to this book as well.

> This book will emphasize some key principles of the soul that need to be appropriated to be changed. But it all begins with your relationship with God. Most life change occurs alone with God. Don't miss this. Only God changes the heart. Only God heals the soul. Only God sets the captives free. Many churches today have one of these components in their culture: anointed truth, true community, or the presence and power of God. But it takes all three to create a culture of deep change. It is equally true of inner healing ministry. The practitioners I have observed who have the greatest, most lasting impact on the people they serve have combined all three of these components into their ministry. All three are necessary for life change. If you are a leader in the church, one of your primary jobs is to create the right kind of culture. Create a culture

where all three components are accessible. If you are a church attender, and all three are not readily visible in your church, then you may need to go to other places to access some of the tools and resources you need for life change.[1]

Please understand that my highest desire is for you to experience the life-changing message that only God's Spirit and His Word can provide. However, in my experience, it takes great work, a lot of effort, tears, frustration, late nights, early mornings, and, finally, much focused attention on changing our old thought patterns and old habits to allow God to facilitate fully the change in hearts. Unfortunately, this type of healing does not usually take place in a moment of high inspiration in a one-and-done church service although it would be wonderful if that would happen and allow us to bypass the healing work and process of the wilderness journey completely.

We simply cannot skip the "middle," move our game piece to the end, and say, "Look, wow, we feel better!" I plead with you not to skip the middle and to continue to pretend, "I'm good; you're good! We're all good."

For true healing to occur, we must submit to the oftentimes painful healing process and allow our minds to become re-wired. Give neuron pathways the opportunity to re-fire and realign as newly born pathways of the Spirit of God and His Word.

This book will provide you with the major steps that make up the framework of liberation from the enemy's hold on your mind. Listen to me, though. As you read, continue to tell yourself, *I am valuable enough to be seen, heard, and healed.*

You must be desperate to escape the pathways your mind has created from years of overuse of toxic thought patterns, misguided beliefs, and misapplied scriptural thinking. "Self-awareness is the gateway to life change. We cannot heal that which we will not admit. God cannot cleanse that which we will not confess."[2]

I can promise you that the easiest method to avoid discomfort will be to abandon this book and toss it into the nearest trash can! Nonetheless, true transformation requires an openness to creating thought processes that arise from carefully written mantras and Scriptures. These will lead you to new neuron networks in the brain. I will be painfully honest; this will not be an overnight miracle. This will be a lengthy work of the Spirit in your life through much prayer, soul searching, and renovation work to the very foundation of your mind and of your life as you know it now.

I plead with you to take this journey. I have walked this road through the murky, muddy waters of the swamp and survived. I really believe you will survive the journey with the Lord's help.

Revelation

Several years ago, I taught a Bible study from my dining room table. The young, single mom I instructed brought joy to my heart as she absorbed the Word of God eagerly. She asked splendid yet tough questions, and I had to be ever ready for her inquisitive mind. One day as I taught her the Word while entertaining her two little girls with toys from the living room stash, something amazing happened. I had been presenting the *Search For Truth 2* Bible study and began to read aloud from Genesis 3 how Eve lost her original dominion and authority due to her ever-reaching and colossal mistake.

The young mom said, "Well, Eve didn't die, did she? God had said they would die if they ate the fruit. So what does that mean?"

I thought, *Well, you're not wrong,* but didn't have a more conclusive answer for her since I also had wondered about that very fact for pretty much my entire life. I did what any good Bible study teacher would do and suggested, "Let's keep going, and maybe we will find that answer later in the Bible study."

As I continued to teach, I received a strong revelation of a truth that made total sense to me. I finally realized what the Bible meant when it mentioned a person's spirit, soul, and body.

When Eve ate the piece of fruit in the Garden of Eden and shared it with her husband that pivotal day, sin broke man's communion with God, and the couple stood as sinners for the first time in the known world. From that day to today, we humans have been dealing with

16

Eve's transgression and the resulting tumble of mankind into sin. From the moment Eve ate the fruit in the garden, her innocence was lost and judgment ensued. This began a broken relationship with a pattern of alienation from God and isolation from God. Sadly, Eve had lost her innocence, and she could do nothing to regain that.

The revelation I received identified the soul and the spirit. We humans are generously given charge of two-thirds of this equation since we have the charge of our souls and bodies. Of the two, though, our soul is the only thing we "own." While we are the guardians or stewards of our bodies, our "temples" as the New Testament explains it, our bodies belong to God who created them. The spirit is driven by God or sin.

Another way to look at the meaning of our soul unfolds in the BibleProject and its series of videos about the Jewish *Shema*. The BibleProject defines soul with the Hebrew word *nephesh*, which simply means our entire being, life, and body.

> To love God with all your *nephesh* means to devote your whole physical existence to your Creator, the one who granted us these amazing bodies in the first place. It's about offering your entire being with all of its capabilities and limitations in the effort to love God and to love your neighbor as yourself. And that's the Hebrew word for soul.[3]

When we are born, our souls have control of us. Our souls consist of our minds, our wills, and our emotions. We were designed by the Creator to offer our whole physical existence back to the Creator and not to be solely in charge of ourselves, but that is not what happens when sin is involved with God's creation.

Our mind is what we think.
Our will is what we want.
Our emotions are what we feel.

———————

The *Search for Truth 2* study refers to the three parts of man:

17

> Soul: mind, will, and emotions that operate by the five
> senses of seeing, hearing, touching, tasting, and
> smelling. The soul will be ruled by sensual pas-
> sions and desires.
> Body: the house of the building in which the invisible
> spirit and soul live. The body is subject to pain,
> disease, death, and decay.
> Spirit: real inner man, the part that knows God and can
> be separated from God through sin and, there-
> fore, in union with Satan.

Alienation from God points to our need for reconciliation. I had the strong realization that day in my dining room that Eve did not die a physical death, but she suffered a spiritual death immediately. A spiritual death just means that Eve was separated from God, forever cursed. "Since man is a spirit-being, it was into the spirit, created in God's image, that death entered. This does not mean that Adam and Eve ceased to be spirit-beings. Rather than being a state of non-existence, spiritual death is an existence separated and alienated from God."[4] This pattern would continue for hundreds of years until Noah finally found grace in the eyes of the Lord (Genesis 6:8).

When we consider our lives, we are all born sinners. Babies are born sinners, a crazy concept! We can thank Eve for initiating this condition of mankind. Once Adam and Eve yielded to Satan, they lost dominion over the earth and instantly incurred a spiritual death. They became dirty with sin. Adam lived to 930 years, but the moment he ate that fruit, his spiritual man died.

We humans are spirit beings, created in God's image. Our moms and dads hold the responsibility for our physical bodies, but God is responsible for the soul and the spirit. Spiritual death is defined as separation and alienation from God.

18

"**Physical death** separates man's spirit and soul from his body.
"**Spiritual death** separates man's spirit from God."[5]

And you He made alive, who were dead in trespasses and sins, in which you once walked according to the course of this world, according to the prince of the power of the air, the spirit who now works in the sons of disobedience (Ephesians 2:1-2, NKJV).

When our souls wield the power, we are ruled by our human thinking, our human wants, and our human feelings. If we wonder why the world is in such chaos, this should help us realize that our souls lead us into distressing trouble—every day, all day.

God created us to be connected to Him and for our spirits to be controlled and ruled by His Spirit, but sin isolates and alienates us from God. When we are separated from God, we cannot hear God nor can we fully follow God. We cannot please God if we are ruled by our wills, our thoughts, and our emotions.

All of this is nice, but what in the world does it have to do with shame? We must arrive at this important junction in order to comprehend why living in shame is so harmful.

When our souls are in charge, we are separated from God. This is a highly dangerous place to be, even for a short while. Not only did man's spirit die, but his soul (mind, will, emotions) became darkened, subjected to the enemy. He became a child of Satan. Jesus told the self-righteous Pharisees, *Ye are of your father the devil, and the lusts of your father ye will do* (John 8:44, KJV).

> While God's nature is life, Satan's nature is death. We must clearly understand these two words, "life" and "death," in order to accurately comprehend the message of the Bible. Paul wrote,

> "And you hath he quickened, who were dead in trespasses and sins; wherein in time past ye walked according to the course of this world, according to the prince of the power of the air, the spirit that now worketh in the children of disobedience" (Ephesians 2:1-2).

19

"In whom the god of this world hath blinded the minds of them which believe not, lest the light of the glorious gospel of Christ, who is the image of God, should shine unto them (II Corinthians 4:4).

Spiritual death is as real as life. The difference is that death comes from Satan and life from God. All that is good, beautiful, and holy originates from God. All that is evil, bad, and corrupt comes from the devil. Satan's nature began to rule in the spirit of man when spiritual death seized dominion over creation."[6]

In the New Testament, the apostle Paul wrote extensively about our consciences. Our spirits are the God-conscious places where God talks to us. If we hold a continual grudge against ourselves, we have likely separated from God since we are not connected to Him. We cannot be soul-controlled and Spirit-controlled simultaneously. Either we are God-controlled, or our human souls hold the seat of power.

> There are only two thrones: Righteousness and Unrighteousness.
> —Mark Morgan

The Bible speaks often of our souls. Within the writings of Proverbs, we learn to guard our souls, knowing that to a hungry soul, even bitter things are sweet. Proverbs 25:28 counsels that we have to keep our human spirits, or our souls, ruled well, or we will become like a city with broken walls. This simply means that anything has direct access to us if our soul/spirit walls have fallen.

As we entertain toxic thoughts and harmful patterns, we remain in a cycle that usually repeats itself for a lifetime unless healing happens. Dr. James Hughes explains that our brains cannot stand confusion. In what we say, think, and do, it is imperative that the actions of the spirit, soul, and body are in sync, not in continual disequilibrium. When we live with toxic shame 24/7, our brains remain in constant confusion because we are not living what we know. While we fail to live what our spirits tell us, our bodies suffer the consequence of constant stress.

The *Search for Truth 2* Bible study elaborates:

Let's see how each part of man was affected by the terrible death nature after Adam sinned against God.

Sin affects the spirit. God's plan was that He would rule man's spirit and man's spirit would control the soul and body. God's world would then be governed and subdued by those who were themselves governed by God.

But man wanted to be like God and would not remain under His sovereignty. Consequently, Adam's spirit suffered the worst punishment of all. He lost contact with his Maker.

No longer could Adam enjoy the daily fellowship of God's presence. Worse still, he became partners with the rebel forces led by Satan.

Sin affects the soul. With the spirit now dead, the soul took charge. From the cradle to the grave, man is controlled by his "soulish" mind, will, and emotions. Spiritual concepts are foreign to him. To have faith in the unseen, intangible promises of God's Word is very difficult. He lives only by what his sense [five senses] knowledge dictates.

Before Adam sinned, his intelligence was so superb, he was able to name the entire animal creation (Genesis 2:19-20). His mental powers were fully capable of ruling the earth.

But after death seized man, his mind and emotions were captured by fleshly passions and desires. Medical science now believes that few people use more than ten percent of their brainpower.

Sin affects the body. Adam was created with physical perfection and endless life. His strong, healthy body was suitable to house the creature who would fellowship with his Creator and have dominion over the earth.

21

However, spiritual death changed all that. Adam became a *mortal*, which means "death-doomed" or "Satan-ruled." Having become enslaved by death, he became susceptible to pain, disease, and sickness.

From the moment of birth, we begin that long, slow process of dying. When at last the body ceases to function, decay proceeds to dismantle and reduce the lifeless form to its original substance—dirt.[7]

What does all this mean? I mean, we aren't dead yet, we go to church, we pray and read our Bibles, and the list goes on, right? In the church, we have many phrases that basically mean nothing to any of us. We have heard them for so long they are like wallpaper in our minds—there but not heard. Some of those phrases are:

"They're in the flesh."

"Just be Spirit-led."

"Don't act like the world."

"Just move on."

"That's past, so forget about it."

On and on we go with the empty platitudes that help no one.

On the day of the revelation, I pondered all I had learned and what I must unlearn. I realized that being in my flesh equals acting according to my soul, which means my mind, will, and feelings are in control rather than God. I also grasped that people in the world's system have only their souls by which to live as they are not controlled by God's Spirit. Growing up, I was led to believe that "the world" represented a terrible and undesirable place. That is true, for the Word calls us to be of this world but not controlled by the world.

When we truly have a revelation of who God is in the world and who we are in the world, we will be radically changed forever! I fervently wish that all of us would slow down enough to comprehend these things, some we have ignored for too long.

What if we didn't just slow down our bodies, what if we chose to slow down all of us, our souls included? It's time we slowed down our [hearts, minds, and] souls. The time has come for us to surrender so that we can take back control of our lives. Because there is power in letting go and resilience in that pause.[8]

As Elevation Worship sings in their song "My Testimony," Jesus has moved us from the place of death's control into the life of justification as He reigns in our spirits.

Reflection

1. Why is the entire world in chaos?
2. How do we regain the dominion that was lost in Genesis 3?
3. What does it mean to be soul-led? Spirit-led?
4. Do you:
   Understand how dominion was lost in Genesis 3 and how to recover that dominion?
   Understand the multitude of tragic consequences resulting from Adam's willful sin that have forever affected mankind and his world?
   Understand the spirit, soul, and body connection?
5. Who is in charge of you—God or you? Do you know?
6. Have you considered being Spirit-led, and are you aware of how this happens?
7. Take a moment to journal what you understand about the soul and spirit connection. This is vitally important as we proceed in this book.

Stolen Identity

Growing up, we lived outside town, in the country, complete with dusty dirt roads and winding creeks. We lived in a trailer house surrounded by green pastures populated by several horses and brown cows with giant, woeful brown eyes. We had corrals, barns, creeks, hayfields, and a long driveway. As we drove that lane at night, the cows would stare at our car. A porch ran the length of the trailer house, and that concrete slab became my and my sister's bicycle race-track. Several things transpired in that trailer house that forged lasting memories in me.

A tragic accident occurred in our extended family, and one of my cousins was on life support due to a terrible truck wreck. My family spent quite a bit of time at the hospital with the family as we waited on God to heal my cousin from his extensive brain injury. Finally, the terrible news came that God had other plans for my cousin. Once the life-saving machines were turned off, it was just a matter of time before he passed into glory. Either this night or the evening of his funeral, something happened that embedded in my memory.

That evening, we arrived at the trailer house only to find it ransacked. Everything was torn apart. The front door had been pried open and stood ajar in the dark, cold night. In the barn, numerous articles had been turned upside down. In addition, the perpetrator had stolen our saddles and bridles.

I was only a little girl, but I remember the awful feeling that came over me. I realized that some unknown person had come into our little house and had taken more than stuff. He had taken my security and my sense of safety within my own home. For years, I was afraid of coming home to a dark house. In the end, the thief had stolen much more from me than just stuff. He had stolen my confidence that the world was a good place and that people were mostly good.

To this day, I have had to reclaim the emotional and spiritual items that were stolen. While I cannot remember if any of our personal belongings were ever returned, I do recall the loss and the wave of powerlessness that overcame me as I stood surveying the damage.

This story makes me realize that for many of us, the enemy of our souls has taken much more than bridles, saddles, and stuff. This same enemy has returned time and again to the soul door left ajar in our emotional states and has stolen us blind. What makes me so upset is our own feelings of inadequacy and shame have allowed him access to our most valuable possessions.

We have allowed the enemy to reclaim territory that was handed back to us by Jesus Christ as He was beaten at the whipping post and as He hung on the wooden cross. Yes, in Genesis 3, Adam and Eve's identity, dominion, and authority were taken from them due to their rebellion. Satan would love for us to remain in the place of weakness and fear due to shame and toxic thinking. Most of us are no match for anything Satan tries to tell us. We give too much credit to the poor ol' devil! That scum wad gets much more press and time on the board than he deserves.

> There can be no transformation where there is no revelation. We cannot overcome that which we will not admit. —Rob Reimer

Without realizing this, we have permitted our identities for our emotional, spiritual, and mental states to be stolen. God has clearly told us who we are in Him through His Word, but through years of toxicity and old thought patterns, we have allowed a false image to ID us. This stolen identity concept is multifaceted. Most of us have no idea who we are and, beyond that, seriously have zero idea of who we are in Christ. Your identity in Christ is the foundation for a healthy soul and spirit. Who you are determines how you behave.

To make my point a bit further, ask anyone you know this question: "Who are you in Christ?" I have asked this question to folks, and they usually stammer and stutter as they attempt to come up with an answer. It's such a sad reality for all of us really, but we will figure it out by the end of this book. I promise!

═══════════════════════

First, we must have a revelation of who Christ is to us. Then, we have a revelation of who we are in Christ, our true identity according to the Scriptures. Finally, we see where we belong in the kingdom of God and recognize our unique gifts and callings.

Here are a few questions to make sure we really understand this amazing concept of identity.

✦ Who is God?
✦ Who is God to you?
✦ Could you explain who God is to you without your Bible?
✦ Have you ever considered who you are in Christ and what you do in the kingdom?

Many people do not know who they are in Christ. Thus, they miss the reason they live on this earth. For many years, I had the mistaken thought that identity in Christ was defined by my role in ministry or in life at that moment. If you had asked me about my identity in Christ many years ago, I would have given replies such as these:

Wife
Mom
Daughter & sibling
Pastor's wife
Sectional youth leader's wife
Teacher
Van driver
Youth camp worker
Neighborhood friend

My identity in Christ was completely wrapped up in the titles and roles of my life. I first heard Terry and Melani Shock present this concept in an Oklahoma Ministers' Retreat several years back. Their session rocked my world once I realized that I had tangled my identity in Christ and my kingdom purpose all together into one huge, knotted mess!

Painfully, I started on the journey of trying to figure out who I am in Christ and who Christ intends me to be through His Word. Then I could tackle the hardest part: my kingdom purpose, the reason God placed me on this earth.

Most people cannot answer this tough query, "What problem were you put on this earth to solve?" Someone asked me that a few months ago, and I was stumped. Completely stumped. I could not answer the question. I prayed. I thought. I journaled. I sat in my glider chair and rocked as I pondered this question. I walked outside, up and down the road. I distracted myself from thinking about the question with all sorts of piddling jobs and had a sudden yet intense preoccupation with trivial yet apparently important assignments like vacuuming the floors and cleaning countertops.

Satan has been so thorough with his game of "steal, kill, and destroy" that most people living for the Lord just trudge through life with their heads down, merely existing through each day. Most of them begrudge the passing of time and their lack of time but never seem to do anything to make drastic changes. I would venture as far as to say that most of you dread each day and don't awaken with joy most mornings. Why is this?

Who are we, and what were we created to accomplish on this earth? Merely to exist to drink more bougie coffee tomorrow morning? To attend one more church service where we promptly forget the sermon and hardly, if ever, make the application to our lives?

God created each person with a specific purpose. He designs every individual to be a standout for the kingdom and to accomplish something that no other person can do. Each of us is unique, and no one else can come close to doing what each of us has been called by God to accomplish.

Ephesians 4:15 tells us to speak the truth in love and to grow up in every way into Him, who is the head, Christ. When will we grow up and into our gifts and callings? If not now, when?

Kingdom purpose and God's callings sometimes get twisted up in titles and roles. A person might be a mother or a father, but that is not her or his kingdom purpose. We all realize that being a mother is the highest calling for a woman to fulfill, but that isn't the only purpose a woman ought to fulfill for God's kingdom.

Kingdom purpose is the one thing that each person must fulfill on this earth. Purpose is why we exist. Purpose is what God tailor-made each of us to do in this life. If someone were to do something drastic such as putting her spiritual gifts into action, people would mock her about a mid-life crisis. Nonetheless, she would walk in purpose.

Reimer asserts, "Your identity in Christ is the foundation of a healthy soul. Who you are determines how you behave. What you believe about yourself influences your level of maturity, peace, and soul health." The time has come for you to stop believing the lies you have believed for so long and to understand truly who you are in Christ. You can begin behaving in that direction, believing good things about yourself, and expecting your personal efforts to accomplish mighty victories for the kingdom of God.

Let me explain something before many of you push the off-go-away-now button on your book remote. We all must grasp that God's Word has several universal purposes for each of us to fulfill. We find these throughout the Bible, but we will focus on three.

Deuteronomy 6:4-5 states the first universal purpose. In this passage, God commanded the Israelites to love God with a singleness of heart. Because there is only one God, they were commanded to love Him with their entire heart, soul, strength, and mind. Moses went on to instruct the body of believers to teach their families about this one God every day: morning, noon, and night.

The second universal purpose is found in all four Gospels. Many like to quote only Matthew 28:18-19 as the Great Commission, but

Jesus' words are found in every Gospel as well as in the beginning of Acts. Jesus, while He gave His final instructions to the few disciples gathered with Him on the Mount of Olives, left us another command or purpose. Jesus instructed everyone to teach and baptize people in the name of the Lord Jesus Christ. This purpose applies to everyone who lives on the earth, so we understand its universal nature.

We find the third universal purpose in Mark 12:30-31. Here we are instructed to love God and to love people. These two seemingly simple commands turn out to be two of the toughest things we will do in our lives. The only thing tougher to do is to love ourselves, but we will get to that soon enough.

Foundation Renovation

I started the book with "stolen identity" because the likelihood that you—or any of us, really—truly understand your kingdom purpose at this point is tiny. Though some of you might be rock stars and have known your true calling and purpose for the kingdom since you were two years old, the overwhelming majority of us have not.

Matthew 10:8 presents a concept of giving what we possess. We can give only what we possess. We cannot give what we do not have. Most Christians are so filled with self-loathing and confusion that they have no idea of who they are in Christ or what they were put on this earth to achieve. If you cannot discover your value through God and His Word, you will not become what you are supposed to be through Him. No matter how big God is, how I view myself in God determines how I will live in Him.

"Two lies will lock you up and you cannot get out or free on your own: Lies and Unforgiveness. If you believe the lies you will act on those lies and then the lies will trap you. Unforgiveness traps quicker than anything else" (Dr. James Hughes).

Please do not allow this to make you feel worse about yourself. That will only complicate what we are working on here. The main reason you are reading this book is to figure out how to stop the lies in your mind and to begin inching your way toward freedom. That liberty will propel you forward, into the specific kingdom design that God has for you.

Reimer stated, "Self-awareness is the gateway to life change." Right now, I invite you to begin an introspection into your life and inner person that will require some renovation to the foundation. Any time a building is erected, the foundation is laid first. We have all seen skyscrapers in the process of construction. It seemed the work below the ground with the tall cranes lasted many months. The engineers were establishing a foundation that would withstand the height and weight of the enormous edifice.

Wikipedia tells us that the tallest tower in the world right now is located in Dubai, United Arab Emirates. Construction started on the Burj Khalifa Tower in 2004 and was not completed until 2009. Five years! The tower has 154 floors and 57 elevators and is just over a half-mile tall. I am curious how long the crew worked on the foundation underground before they started construction on the part above the ground that we can see.

Our lives must be like this skyscraper that was built with so much attention to the foundation of reinforced concrete and structural steel. How much attention have we given to the foundational aspects of our lives? Can our current foundation support our kingdom purpose? Can our life continue with limited foundational support, or is our building leaning dangerously to the side, like the Leaning Tower of Pisa? Is our building crumbling, or has it already fallen down completely? If a hurricane came through right now, would it take out your already damaged building?

Have you said these things to yourself recently?

+ I am no good.
+ I am flawed and hopeless.
+ I am not sure that God even loves me.
+ I am wasting my time here.
+ It doesn't matter anyway.
+ I can't help it.
+ I am good for nothing.

31

Have you noticed that your thoughts and behavior don't match? What is underneath your behavior? What motive do you have for your actions each day? Why do you do what you do? Are you working to repair from the ground up or merely working to alleviate the symptoms? Are you mostly concerned with your behavior only and trying to fix what you think is wrong with your actions without renovating the foundation?

Our lives are filled with chaos often because we are living out the prophecy we believe about ourselves, as Dr. James Hughes explains. This becomes a self-fulfilling prophecy, for Solomon wrote, *As [a man] thinks in his heart, so is he* (Proverbs 23:7).

During the writing of this manuscript, I read in the Book of Judges one morning, and the first few chapters really spoke to me. God had said that He purposefully left some of the nations in Canaan unconquered by Joshua. The enemies would test the Israelites to see if they would serve the Lord. They failed the test. God's chosen people chose to follow the Amorites and all of the "ites" when they imitated the moral corruption and child sacrifice. The Israelites were trapped in a cycle of rebellion and sin, suffering, oppression, repentance, and deliverance.[9]

One could enumerate many reasons why the Israelites were in this cycle of sin and repentance. For our purposes, let's just say they were so caught up in the culture of the new country that they soon forgot what God had already done for them. In how many ways does this parallel with the modern church? Whew!

Still, a question arises: Have we taken on more of the culture than we are supposed to? Since many of our great elders have passed on to their reward, has God left us unconquered things to test us with our allegiance and loyalty to Him and His ways?

This made me wonder how the great elders of our day made it through their lives without succumbing to the culture and to shame. When I think about these great people—Nona Freeman, a powerful missionary to Africa; J. T. Pugh, mighty preacher and molder of men;

Billy Cole, international evangelist and crusade preacher—I wonder how they accomplished so much in their lifetimes and how they pushed through the feelings of inadequacies and shame. What about Oma Ellis and Willie Johnson? Murrell Ewing and James Kilgore?

While I don't have a great answer, I am fairly sure they had a rock solid foundation of absolute faith in God and a knowledge of how God works. Also, most importantly, they knew who they were in God. Identity. They had an overriding kingdom purpose. While they all experienced seasons of trust busts, I am sure they somehow marched steadfastly forward in their calling and gifts. The apostle Paul told us in I Corinthians 15:58 to be unshakeable and unmoveable. These elders obviously demonstrated that verse to us.

But how do we get to where they were? How did those elders develop such a strong sense of purpose and identity in God that they were immune to the culture and to the lies of the enemy? While I don't really have exact answers about those elders, I am certain they had a strong sense of who they were in Christ. Nothing in life or from the enemy could shake that strong foundation.

Stolen or Lost?

While many reasons lie behind the identity that has been lost or stolen from you, the most valuable thing you can hear me say right now is that you do have purpose and hope. Our culture wants us to continue to speak things over ourselves such as:

- ✦ "I am feeling really anxious."
- ✦ "I am just so stressed out."
- ✦ "This day is just getting worse."
- ✦ "What's next?"
- ✦ "I just had a panic attack."

As you continue to read, pay attention to the words your mind tells you. These words are not your boss, and most likely, the words are not true. Shauna Niequist described her messed-up identity best.

33

I believed that I was fine, that I was a workhorse, that I didn't need special treatment or babying, or self-care. Self-care is for the fragile, the special, the dainty. I was a linebacker, a utility player, and a worker bee. I ate on the run, slept in my clothes, worshiped at the altar of my to-do list, and ignored the crying out of my body and soul like they were nothing more than pesky mosquitoes.[10]

The feelings that accompany these words also feel true, but most of the time, feelings are real but are not true. Awareness of the words and the lies in your mind will begin the healing.

Let's take a few baby steps today toward healing. You might not see the progress as much, but you are here. You are reading. You are beginning to have hope and are on the road to healing. Either we go on as we always have, slowly eroding and becoming unrecognizable while stealing from ourselves everything God has promised us, or we made the hard and fast decision right now to seek a new pathway. We have the chance to seek God's redemption for allowing this thievery in the first place.

From here, we will begin a complete inspection of the foundation of your life's structure. Most likely, you will need a complete renovation of the foundation, complete with foundation jacks and structural specialists. The really great news is that in a few months, your foundation will be much stronger, capable of withstanding much more pressure and wind speeds. Your skyscraper structure will be solid. You will be able to add many floors to the foundation, which will result in a gorgeous new structure.

My Friend Who Didn't Know

A few years back, I lost a dear friend. She was the epitome of a great mom and all things household. She was the wife of a minister, pastor, and evangelist. Her before-Christ days had been filled with all sorts of addiction to every type of drug and every bottle of alcohol available at that time. To say her testimony was amazing is a huge understatement. Several times, I heard her give her testimony. Each time, people were delivered from all sorts of addiction and mightily transformed by the powerful witness of God's Spirit after she spoke.

Even though she had a great family, support system, local church, and network of caring friends, she began to struggle with hormonal symptoms. At some point, she began her descent into a deep depression. At first, her thinking was dysfunctional and distorted. I would talk to her for hours and text back and forth, to no avail. At some point, she isolated herself and refused to speak to anyone from her support system. Paranoia struck, followed by hallucinations. Tragically, after several months of increased mental turmoil, she took her own life.

To say I was devastated would be a mild description of what I felt, not to mention the effects on her husband and family, who were blindsided by their own grief. My first thoughts were: *We weren't able to do enough. We couldn't reach her. We should've done more to try to help her.* As I prayed, wept, and sought the Lord, He spoke something heart-wrenching that I shall not forget.

My daughter did not heed My voice. She went her own way. She chose her destruction. I loved her. I had a work for her to do but she refused to heed or believe. She could not believe she was worthy or called of Me. Do not go this way. Listen to Me. Always. I will instruct you. I will show you how to go and the way to go. Talk to others. Urge them to believe Me. I am the only way. Walk therein. Believe Me, as others have not.

With a heavy heart, I share this with you. I sadly now know that my friend had unresolved shame. She never could believe that she was worthy of the call of God on her life, her kingdom purpose. Her identity had been so completely stolen from her that she lost herself in herself.

Since the Lord instructed me to tell others and urge others to believe Him, that is exactly what I am trying to do here. I implore you, please listen to the Lord as He speaks to you. Please remove all un-resolved shame so that you begin this moment to rediscover your mighty kingdom purpose. The kingdom is awaiting your first move. Please honor my friend and begin your journey of healing.

Lauren Daigle beautifully shares this struggle in her song, "You Say." Though voices in our minds condemn and belittle us, Jesus says we are His, we are loved, and we have worth in Him. His voice has greater authority than any other when we choose to listen.

Reflection

1. Who are you? Who is God to you?
2. Who are you in Christ? Do you know?
3. What has the enemy stolen from you? What lies about your-self have you believed?
4. The song I referenced says that in Christ we find our worth and our identity. How is this true for you?
5. What is the source of your worth?
6. For the lies you have believed, locate a verse of Scripture that says the opposite. Insert your name into the verse and pray that Scripture for the next month or so.

Shame Assessment

Please prayerfully work through this shame assessment. Only when we truly allow ourselves to assess ourselves, will we begin the healing process of escaping the swamp.

1. I feel that I hear the still, small voice of God:
   o Daily.
   o Often.
   o Never.
2. I feel that something is blocking me from God's presence and/or voice.

○ Yes, I feel very blocked from God.

○ No, I hear God's voice each day.

3. I have heard about this stuff before, but I am:

  ○ Not sure if I have shame.

  ○ Pretty sure I have shame.

  ○ I am certain that I have worked to remove my issues and my shame, and I feel redeemed every day.

4. When I think about personally presenting the gospel to someone or praying for someone outside the church walls, I have the feeling that:

  ○ I am not good enough to tell someone about the Lord.

  ○ I have issues and am not sure how to resolve them, so I don't feel I could lead someone to Christ.

  ○ I am fearful that I won't say or pray the right thing. What if I mess up?

5. I have so many unresolved issues that I cannot seem to get past, and those issues make me feel unsuccessful in the kingdom of God.

  ○ Yes

  ○ No

  ○ Maybe

6. Every day, I am plagued by feelings of extreme regret or embarrassment over my past, lack of accomplishment, or even present junk.

  ○ Yes

  ○ No

7. I hear people talk about being free in Jesus, but I am not sure I am free.

  ○ Yes, I feel the heaviness and don't feel peace often.

  ○ No, I am free in Jesus and have peace almost every day.

8. I condemn myself on a regular basis with hurtful words, such as: "I'm not good enough. If only people knew who I really am! Jesus hasn't really forgiven me for what I said or did when. . . . Jesus doesn't really love me because. . . . I am unworthy and cannot seem to do enough to please God or

other people. Self, why can't you just get your life together?"
- o   Yes, every day
- o   No, never happens to me
9. I can truly say that I love myself. I can say that I live my life as an open book, not at all concerned about who really knows me, my past, my stuff, and so on.
    - o   Yes, absolutely, my life is an open book.
    - o   No, I am terrified that people might find out about something I have hidden or not told anyone.
    - o   I am working on being authentic and vulnerable with my brothers, sisters, and elders in Christ although it is still a bit tough for me.
10. I am fearful of:
    - o   Not ever reaching my potential in Christ.
    - o   Someone finding out that I have issues.
    - o   My mind and emotions having control rather than the Spirit of God.
    - o   All of the above.
11. I constantly feel like I have a grudge against myself; I don't really like me all that much. How could I ever do anything for the kingdom?
    - o   Yes—oh, my goodness—that is me!
    - o   No, I know that I am a mighty woman of God and I have a purpose to fulfill.
12. I am certain that God unconditionally loves me for me.
    - o   Of course!
    - o   Well, if I did XYZ or something else, then God would love me for me.

When you have finished the assessment, look at your responses. How many responses indicate shame? There is no scoring grid for this assessment. This is only a tool to help you break through the clutter inside your head and see something concrete about where you are right now with unresolved shame.

Journey into the Swamp

"You cannot defeat darkness by running from it, nor can you conquer your inner demons by hiding them from the world. In order to defeat the darkness, you must bring it into the light."
—Seth Adam Smith

A scary childhood memory came from a swamp right below our house. Yes, I realize that we grew up in eastern Oklahoma, but just work with me and my overactive imagination. That corner of the yard was always wet and had a swamp-like appearance, complete with sturdy cattails that were always taller than us kids. This swamp was at the bottom of the hill where we walked to and from the bus. That swamp always intrigued me as I imagined all sorts of ferocious beasts and creatures inside those tall brown tips and green leaves surrounded by the unruly weeds that the lawnmower never seemed to reach.

Recently, I drove by this childhood home, and the swamp was gone with no evidence it had ever existed. I was sad but also realized something amazing. Just as I had always imagined scary monsters lurking beneath those tall plants, I never knew if the monsters truly existed. Just driving by the yard again brought some relief to my ten-year-old imagination. The swamp was gone, which meant there were no more scary beasts that could jump out and drag me into the depths of the mire at the base of the yard.

Many times, we create swamps in our minds. Our swamps likely have imagined beasts right out of a thriller movie. Swamps are thick, gooey bogs that trap our minds with little hope of escape! In some circles, shame is often defined as the swampland of the soul.

39

Usually, we would like to bypass the swamp or run around it in wild circles. Instead, we are going to wade in and struggle our way through the bog and the possibility of what we might find lurking in the depths. How do we get trapped in these swamps, and how do we find the way out? We need to take courage and trek into the murky swamp to figure out what scary beasts are there and how to slay them once and for all.

> Incongruent living is exhausting.
> —Brené Brown

Remember the remark Dr. James Hughes made about our minds disliking confusion? We really desire to be right and do right, but the boggy swamp gets the best of us. We end up living in a way we know we shouldn't, but we don't know how to make the changes we need. It's an exhausting way to live for sure!

Living with cognitive dissonance is harmful to our bodies, especially to our actual brains. The nerves in our brains unplug when we tell ourselves to stop or to do something different than we're doing but we keep going anyway. If we continue to overwrite our brains, our frontal lobe will be completely rewired in a few months.

When the Bible speaks of a seared conscience, it just means that the person's brain was finally and completely unplugged.[11] This results from living with incongruence between our minds and our actions in a negative fashion for years.

> *I don't really understand myself, for I want to do what is right, but I don't do it. Instead, I do what I hate. But if I know that what I am doing is wrong, this shows that I agree that the law is good. So I am not the one doing wrong; it is sin living in me that does it. And I know that nothing good lives in me, that is, in my sinful nature. I want to do what is right, but I can't. I want to do what is good, but I don't. I don't want to do what is wrong, but I do it anyway* (Romans 7:15-19, NLT).

Obviously, Paul and the Roman church knew something about incongruence as well.

God knows if we get our hearts healthy, and rightly aligned with Him, our behaviors will follow. But if we get our behaviors in line without dealing with the condition of our hearts, we will become Pharisees at best. We will be left with dark places in the soul and a life full of judgment, not love.[12]

This quote reverberates with the sounds of scary music to me. Forcing our behavior to be in line without renovating the foundation of our soul and spirit leads to darker destinies.

The Benevolent Order of the Approval Addict

The club is officially the Benevolent Order of the Approval Addict. It's not overly picky or elite, accepting participants from every culture, body shape and size, and personality, both male and female. This club is simple to get into. As a matter of fact, everyone in the club is duped into thinking he or she has exclusive rights to the club and that no one else is in the club. Yet there are millions in the club. The funny thing is that no one speaks of membership in the club. All members must remain silent and think they're all alone while they're surrounded by thousands of members acting exactly like them.

While we are in the club, terrible things happen to us. We lose all touch with our inner wisdom and intuition. From about age six, we are kept in hiding from our true selves, and our greatest fears become an unkempt appearance, bad hair, problematic everything, anger, hysteria, lack of coolness, failure to remain current with the style, and similar terrors. This club has a fierce rule and never intends for us to escape its clutches.

Approval Addiction

What is it? This intense desire drives you to obtain approval or to avoid rejection from other people.

41

Approval is like a killer drug. Approval becomes addictive in like manner to controlled or illegal substances. You begin to value the beliefs, opinions, and needs of others more than your own. Receiving disapproval is painful. Your entire decision-making process is overtaken by your need for approval from others. You sacrifice your own dreams and ambitions in order to have the approval of people.

"This addiction is one of the most insidious forms of mind clutter and leaves most people exhausted, trying to 'be all to all people' " (Amy Pearson).

Approval addiction leads us to a dangerous place like a junkie entices a person with a compulsive habit. It functions just like a drug dealer does. The desire to gain approval or to avoid rejection results in certain behaviors or characteristics:

✦ Approval can be anything from a simple smile, positive feedback, or a job promotion to a "like" on social media.
✦ Rejection could be anything from criticism, a funny look, or silent treatment to physical violence.
✦ Resentment emerges when all that hard work doesn't yield the praise and admiration you expected.
✦ You grow overwhelmed because you continue to take on more and more.
✦ You feel miserable in a life that may seem "perfect" to the outside world but sure doesn't feel that way.
✦ You have a lack of achievement.
✦ You have a lack of personal fulfillment.
✦ You suffer from low self-esteem and can produce no confidence in yourself.
✦ Stress increases.
✦ You change your position if someone appears to disapprove.
✦ You pay insincere compliments to gain approval.
✦ You feel upset or worried when someone disagrees with you.

If we don't learn how to be authentic believers who act according to the Word of God, we will war against each other. We will tear each

42

other apart. We become mean people, fighting flesh instead of fighting in the spiritual realm. Our greatest fear is appearing less than perfect and feeling acutely vulnerable. The Epistles are chock-full of passage that tell us how to live, but so many times, we just continue to ignore and perhaps pretend that we don't know the Scriptures are there and pertain to us.

The root problem is we don't feel safe being ourselves. Some are people pleasers or constantly seek achievement and strive to be the best at everything. This leads to confusion in the brain and soul, which eventually leads to stress and, consequently, an increase of cortisol in the body.

Addicts try to control how others see them by changing the way they appear to the outside world. We hide the parts of ourselves that are not okay and are never willing to risk vulnerability to get the help we need to overcome those weaknesses. Addictions are tricky because they cover the true root that cries to be healed. One cannot grow when one cannot participate in life. Ephesians 5:13-14 says that when anything is exposed to light, it becomes visible. Our soul usually stops at the age we begin to escape life through addictions or substance abuse. We get stuck at that age until we seek healing.

If you worry about what other people think of you, then you will have more confidence in their opinion than you have in your own. Poor is the man whose future depends on the opinions and permission of others. Remember this, if you are afraid of criticism, you will die doing nothing.[13]

One Sunday morning, our young son was difficult as usual, being strong-willed about getting dressed for church. I was completely depleted and completely at odds with myself before we arrived at the church building. The night before, I had cleaned and worked to have every room of the tiny church building completely perfect for the weekend service before I left. This was all part of the perfect life I thought I was living.

We entered the church through the side door near the driveway. I had not noticed any cars in the back lot and mistakenly thought we were the only people in the building. When I walked into the first classroom carrying our red-faced and still defiant two-year-old, I was immediately taken aback by the huge mess on the table. My first clue should have been the overhead projector that was on and shining onto the wall, but I went into a rage and started shrieking. "What in the world? I cleaned this room last night! What are these people thinking anyway? Who did this? This is such a mess! This makes me so mad!"

I went on and on in my rage until I managed to walk into the next room. What I noticed next brought instant tears to my eyes. The teacher, whom God had sent to help us in the very small church we were attempting to grow, sat in tears with her head bowed. I realized that my raging had completely deflated her and caused her to feel wholly rejected and terribly wounded.

I immediately fell to my knees in front of her and attempted to salvage the morning by begging for forgiveness. While I cried and wailed and tried in vain to explain myself and my horrible morning, I probably only made things worse and made her morning terrible. This event is deeply etched into my long-term memory as an example of rage, anger, and perfection gone so wrong. I was more worried about the church looking perfect and "good" to everyone than I was concerned about my behavior and relationship with the lovely, amazing people God had sent our way.

To protect ourselves, some of us act in these ways:

+ Rehearse what we're going to say—over and over.
+ Mentally go over everything we said or did after a social function to find all the ways we could have done things differently and better, forever overthinking.
+ Apologize constantly.
+ Change the things we do and say depending on whom we are with at the time.
+ Keep our opinions to ourselves when they're not the same opinions as those around us.

- ✦ Assume we know what someone is thinking about us.
- ✦ Work ourselves to death trying to please and making sure everyone around us is happy.
- ✦ Think that our success or happiness depends on the opinions of others.
- ✦ Believe taking time for ourselves—or our spirituality—is a waste of time.

Yes, we ought to do the best we can for God. We are supposed to feel needed and to feel safe. The core problem is when we disconnect from our true selves to get approval or to avoid rejection and we settle for a false sense of belonging.

Approval junkies look outward instead of inward! In that state, we unplug from the Lord, lose our spirit connection, and try to take care of every circumstance through our own strength, personality, or power. In other words, we employ our soul power. We value looking good over our own personal values, our convictions and morals.

These people live in a semi-destroyed state that is consumed by culture, social media, and ego. Multitudes of people have a false sense of belonging to the body of Christ. Outwardly, they seem content and happy. But follow them and listen to them. These backbiting, unsafe people are constantly in a competition with their friends and family members. Always looking to see if someone else is getting ahead, these passive-aggressive people—the judges—make stabs in the form of jokes. "Oh, I'm just kidding." Proverbs has something to say about causing damage and then saying you're only kidding.[14]

Why do these people act so? They have mistakenly thought that their approval comes from their friends and followers on social media instead of from Jesus Christ. They aren't comfortable with who they are in Christ—or don't know who they are in Christ—so they have settled for a false sense of security or a false identity. These people probably have a fear of not pleasing God.

But without faith, it is impossible to please Him, for he who comes to God must believe that He is, and that He is a rewarder of those who diligently seek Him (Hebrews 11:6, NKJV).

45

We mistakenly place our emphasis on what we do for God and for others. Mistakenly, we think that living for God is somehow a big contest. We think we will get a trophy for being busy instead of fulfilling the above verse. How do we please the Lord?

We must learn to trust God's Word more than we trust our feelings. We do not live by emotions; we live by faith. We walk by faith, not by sight (feelings, emotions, human spirit, or will).

It is more important to have a good heart right with God and a less-than-perfect performance than a perfect performance with an impure heart. Many people are called and gifted, but they refuse to budge because they fear they won't be perfect. Some choose to hang on to their issues instead of finding a place of repentance or deliverance. Perfection is and always will be the enemy of obedience.

If the main theme of the entire Bible is obedience, we would be wise to figure out how to be obedient. Words and actions are indeed important. If you ignore or reject God's Word in disobedience, you have alienated yourself from God. In that case, soul-ish behavior will rule your life.

We renew our minds by leaning on God's Word. Then and only then do we begin to think differently.

> *I beseech you therefore, brethren, by the mercies of God, that you present your bodies a living sacrifice, holy, acceptable to God, which is your reasonable service. And do not be conformed to this world, but be transformed by the renewing of your mind, that you may prove what is that good and acceptable and perfect will of God* (Romans 12:1-2, NKJV).

When we sin, we spiritually die. After we have been made alive through the new-birth experience and have been covered by His blood through baptism in Jesus' name, we separate ourselves from God again when we sin. Our soul becomes darkened and subject to the enemy. Adam became a child of Satan the moment he broke the covenant with God. God's nature is life and peace. Satan's nature is death and torment.

According to Mark Morgan, there are only two kingdoms:

- ✦ God or Satan
- ✦ Good or evil
- ✦ Light or darkness
- ✦ Righteousness or iniquity

The beautiful thing is that God allows us the power to choose which kingdom we will be a part of—the power of choice! For so many people, approval addiction is a crime against us. The same people we applaud today will crucify us tomorrow.

━━━━━━━━━━

Several years ago, I stumbled upon an online quiz for approval addiction from Amy Pearson at Be Brazen.[15] Here are the approval-seeking personality categories from the quiz:

- ✦ Perfectionist
- ✦ Scaredy cat
- ✦ Tough guy/gal
- ✦ Hater
- ✦ Performer
- ✦ Chameleon
- ✦ Helper
- ✦ Hero worshiper

Amy Pearson says, "Each of us has an approval seeking persona which is the façade or the mask that we create to obtain the approval of people around us." We do this constantly, daily, to avoid rejection and to seek approval in a sort of soul-ish way that God never planned for us. Jeremiah, the Old Testament prophet, was a member of this order. He was afraid of the people's reactions to his sermons, so God told him to stop watching people's faces and their reactions!

Second Corinthians 10:12-18 directs us not to compare ourselves with others, for when we compare ourselves, we are without understanding. Comparison leads us to more comparison and usually leads us deeper into the swamp.

Brené Brown has said this about perfectionism: "We get sucked into perfection for one very simple reason: We believe perfection will protect us. Perfectionism is the belief that if we live perfect, look perfect, and act perfect, we can minimize pain or avoid the pain or blame, judgment, and shame."[16]

We fear failure because our years of shame and our faulty wiring tell us that we are not good enough and will never be good enough. Therefore, we hold back and never launch that dream or that calling from God. We find ourselves constantly telling everyone how overworked and overtired we are and that we just need more caffeine to make sure that everything is always perfect! (Mother's Day photo booths for local churches on Facebook, anyone?)

Perfectionism and its foul cousin, control, congeal into one huge swamp filled with all sorts of evil and hideous monsters. Sadly, they are all creatures of our own doing. We must simply stop relying on people's opinions and be who we are in Christ. We must drop the pressure to be all, do all, and have it all. This unrealistic pressure is literally killing us!

This book is your invitation to leave the heavy weight of comparison, competition, and exhaustion to be all, have it all, be the part, look the part, have perfect kids and family, and post a perfect life on Instagram. I am inviting you to start over and take a redo on life. Stop long enough to realize that you have been missing true connection, community, and authentic acceptance from the people who love you.

Memory

Memory is the great betrayer. Frequently, as we recall the past, we remember events from the condition of our emotional or soul state at that time. Often my siblings discuss something from our days of childhood or youth. They usually have completely different memories or accounts of occasions than I do. In many cases, I do not remember happenings at all from my early years. I really believe it's because my mind was so busy trying to keep up with the constant confusion that it hindered the storage of important events and stories.

That being said, many of you sweet people reading this book have distinct memories of hurt, wounds, trauma, scars, and other painful events. I am not trying to make light of those painful memories for you. I am only trying to point out that our memories betray us, and our long-term memory is closely connected to our emotions and the capacity for organized thinking at the time of the event.

"The less you talk about it, the more you are motivated by it," declares Brené Brown.

This being said, each of us has memories we have pushed into the recesses of our brains or hearts, and we work very diligently to make sure they never surface. All the while, those memories cause us harm simply because we have not worked to be healed of those events and the people who caused the events. This book is not a counseling book. My purpose is not to work through those memories with you. If you have many memories that keep you in pain, perhaps it is time you locate a safe person with whom to share. Your main goal of sharing or talking over things will be only to be healed and to become a safer person in the future.

The trouble with memory in deep storage is that we continue to go through life spending too much time trying to forget each of those memories. We strive to shut off memories and associations in an effort to numb ourselves. Again, Brené Brown warns us that "we numb everything when we try to shut off negative emotions." As a consequence, many things we can no longer feel, due to our determination to keep everything in the cold, deep darkness of the mind, the swamp.

I heard it put this way: We have things we don't like, so we attempt to push them deep into some dark, cold recess of our heart or soul. The mass is like a poisonous liquid. It could even have been non-poisonous when it was sent to the darkness, but over time, like any living thing left in disrepair for too long, it became moldy and had green specks floating all over the top. We push this down, and then we attempt to smooth something like warm candle wax over the painful substance. Over time, it begins to bubble up again and again. Each time we feel the little bubble, we hurriedly apply more warm candle wax to keep that goo out of sight and out of mind.

This is something else that takes a lot of our time to maintain and to keep hidden. Once again, we have brain confusion each time we spread more warm candle wax on the hurt, the event, the people, and the stuff hidden.

> You can make a drug—a way to anesthetize yourself—out of anything: working out, binge-watching anything, working, shopping, volunteering, cleaning, dieting, codependence in relationships. Any of those things can keep you from feeling pain for a while—that's what drugs do. And, being used like a drug, over time, shopping or TV or work or whatever will make you less and less able to connect to the things that matter, like your own heart and the people you love. That's another thing drugs do: they isolate you.[17]

Just like navigating the swamp, this becomes exhausting and a lot of trouble to continue to maintain. We all must have the grace of God to manage our soul so it doesn't destroy our lives. Remember, toxicity doesn't go away on its own. Toxic thoughts only go away when we yank them out by their roots and replace them with the healing power of the Word of God.

Sovereignty of God

Several years ago, I watched a video of Jeff Arnold, a pastor and bishop in Florida.[18] He made a statement that I resolved to remember. "Some things God ordains that we don't like, like darkness. We discover our weakness in our darkness." Elijah, the Old Testament prophet, became depressed after his greatest day in ministry and went off and hid. Elijah was "anointed and appointed" according to Pastor Arnold. How many of us are anointed and appointed for an amazing kingdom purpose but are still hiding in the darkness of the swamp?

Many times, our time in the swamp doesn't make any sense, but if we ask God to redeem that time we spent in the swamp, I know He will do that. He is a good God and wants to give us only good things.

Pastor Arnold went on to explain that many times our darkness was "not designed to make sense. Rather, God's sovereignty makes saints! We can't make the darkness end and neither can we wish or pray it away."

How many times have we questioned God in the middle of the swamp? At the time, we had absolutely no idea how to get out of the swamp. No matter how long our stay happens to be in the swamp, God does heal, and He doesn't discriminate about those He heals. God made a promise, *I will restore health to you And heal you of your wounds* (Jeremiah 30:17, NKJV).

Trauma

Pain is real. Each of us has different reasons for our pain. I will not try to minimize your pain. I know that God is true, and He is the judge of every one of man's actions on this earth. Someday God will judge each and every word and action of every single person who has ever lived since Adam and Eve. No one will slide by or barely escape the judgment of God. We know that God's Word promises that every knee will bow and every tongue will confess that God is God alone (Romans 14:11).

The church is split on how to deal with hurting people. Those on one side of the issue say that people who struggle emotionally are "in sin." They "Don't have enough faith," "are not obedient," or "don't spend enough time in the Word." These people tend to blame the hurting person for his or her pain. People also say, "God is trying to teach you something." "God is testing you." "Give thanks in spite of your circumstances." These phrases often do not help a person in pain. Often, these phrases make the pain even worse.

The next thing we do is ask, "Is this an emotional problem or a spiritual problem?" If we are struggling with an emotional problem, the Christian psychologist is called in; if it's a spiritual problem, the pastor gets the call. We assume that our depression, panic, guilt, or addictions have little or nothing to do with our spirituality; they are separate issues. But separating our problems into "emotional" problems or "spiritual" problems is part of the problem! All of our problems stem from our failure to reflect the image of God. Because of the fall of Adam and Eve in the Garden of Eden, we have not developed ourselves into the image and likeness of God . . . and we are not functioning as we were created to function. Thus, we are in pain.[19]

A quick reminder about Adam and Eve and the Garden of Eden. They both felt the pain of shame when they sinned. Their sin separated them from God's presence and their relationship with God. Therefore, since the world now had shame and guilt, humans were no longer safe from trauma and pain.

Oftentimes, when we're in pain, we attempt to hide the pain from others. We keep secrets in the dark swamp and work to present our best selves to our friends, family, and church family. Once again, this is a lie we tell ourselves as our minds and our brains slowly struggle with the incongruent life we are trying to live. Dr. Henry Cloud calls this our "false self." He goes on to say that the false self tries to heal itself by its own methods, or as we have learned here, the soul takes over and we do what we want, what we feel, and what we think is right. The whole time, the real us whom God created to become great in His image is swallowed and hidden from view, fully lost inside the dank swamp.

In Ephesians 4:20-25 (NLT), Paul revealed that many of the saints in the church at Ephesus might have been living with the same struggle we face:

But that isn't what you learned about Christ. Since you have heard about Jesus and have learned the truth that comes from him, throw off your old sinful nature and your former way of life, which is corrupted by lust and deception. Instead, let the Spirit renew your thoughts and attitudes. Put on your new nature, created to be like God—truly righteous and holy. So stop telling lies. Let us tell our neighbors the truth, for we are all parts of the same body.

Lies, lies! It is so surprising that the Bible has something to say about living incongruent lives. Spiritual and emotional growth takes time.[20] We must offer grace to ourselves and expect a slow transformative process. Not overnight. Not in one blinding flash of light. One baby step at a time.

Unforgiveness distorts our view of God in a way that is destructive to our faith. Also, many times people with shame loudly declare that they absolutely do not have shame. When we continually harbor ill will and feelings of rage against another person—be it the body of Christ, family, friend, or business co-worker—we remove the blood of Jesus Christ from our lives. In a sense, we remove the only saving blood that has been applied to our lives.

In Colossians 2, we are told to have a circumcision of the heart. In order to have a heart that is right before God, we must set everyone free from the sins committed against us. Rev. James Hughes said, "Confrontation is an act of revenge and passive-aggressive behavior." He added that when our hearts are not right, we become paranoid and refuse to be in community with other believers or friends.

All of this is what happens when we choose to live in the swamp. I said, "Choose." At this point, you're getting an idea of the exact nature of swampish behavior so you can begin to recognize the signs of the shame, the distorted lies, and the toxic thoughts that plague so many people.

When we learn to live authentically, we may look back and give God thanks for the scars that testify to the path that led us to His heart. The group I Am They sings this concept in "Scars." The pain brings wholeness when it brings us to Jesus.

Anyway

People are often unreasonable, illogical, and self-centered;
Forgive them anyway.

If you are kind, people may accuse you of selfish, ulterior motives;
Be kind anyway.

If you are successful, you will win some false friends and some
true enemies;
Succeed anyway.

If you are honest and frank, people may cheat you;
Be honest and frank anyway.

What you spend years building, someone could destroy overnight;
Build anyway.

If you find serenity and happiness, they may be jealous;
Be happy anyway.

The good you do today, people will often forget tomorrow;
Do good anyway.

Give the world the best you have, and it may never be enough;
Give the world the best you've got anyway.

You see, in the final analysis, it is between you and your God;
It was never between you and them anyway.[21]

Reflection

1. How long have you been squishing and mud-bogging in the
    swamp? Do you even remember how or when you arrived at
    the swamp?

2. Which approval behavior(s) do you practice often? Did you realize you had approval addiction? If you were to guess in which category you fit, what would you say: perfectionist, scaredy cat, tough guy/gal, hater, performer, chameleon, helper, or hero worshiper?
3. I didn't say much about hero worship. Nevertheless, in our church culture, I am sadly afraid it is a real thing among us. Journal your thoughts about hero worship in the church and how you handle that pressure and approval behavior.
4. Memory is the great betrayer. Do you agree or disagree? Why?
5. Do you have memories that have betrayed you or that you think might be incorrect in the way you view them?
6. As you read this chapter, did you realize that you have distorted thinking or a memory that might not be correct?
7. Journal your thoughts about any trauma you have faced. You are not alone. Every single person has trauma, hurt, and uncomfortable stuff that has happened to him or her. The important thing is that you bring it out of the swamp so that you and Jesus may begin to discuss it. He will show you how to move forward with His healing power.

Roller Coaster Life

*Y*ou will never rise above your level of self-awareness. The things we deny about ourselves are the very things that deny us from the fullness of God."
—Rob Reimer

Growing up in Tulsa, Oklahoma, we had access to an amusement park called Bells. It was the Taj Mahal of amusement parks to us! If we were so lucky as to visit Bells, we felt we had made it to the big time. Bells had a wooden roller coaster. I remember riding that thing and thinking I would die while, at the same time, believing it was the most exhilarating thing I had ever experienced!

The ups and downs were crazy, but the slow ride to the top of the giant hill was the worst. The clickety-clackety of the cars as we inched to the top of that huge summit made my legs feel like Jello. The suspense took my breath. But when we crested the top of that giant mountain of wood and metal, we screamed for what seemed like days as we rode along the curvy tracks.

At those moments, nothing in life even mattered. We could live right there on the tracks and not remember anything else. Eventually, the ride would end. We would walk to the next ride and repeat the experience over and over.

Little did I know that my life was mirrored in that ride, sometimes terrifyingly fast and sometimes super slow, but always up and down. Up and then down, ever the same cycle. Eventually, I realized that living life on the roller coaster was actually possible even if it wasn't the best way to live.

My Story

For much of my life, I held an intense grudge against myself. I did not like myself and sure didn't love myself. I held the strongest self-hatred you can imagine. I didn't really believe that God could love me for me.

Though I had lived two lives throughout high school and my first year of college, I really thought no one knew. My dad was a pastor, and I had constructed all sorts of scenarios in my mind to justify my actions. I had a list of reasons that I assumed justified the rebellious way I acted. By living this way, I was certain that God wouldn't ever forgive me since I was such a hypocrite.

When my husband first began trying to date me, I did everything I could to push him away. I was mean. I was snarky. I tried all in my power to make him go away. I knew deep inside that I was flawed goods and would never be good enough for the life he would be pursuing. I was smart enough to see that he was headed straight for the ministry, and although I didn't understand all the whys of my actions at that time, I tried everything I could think of to discourage him.

By a long story of God's redemption and longsuffering grace for my hard-headed self, my course changed on a summer youth missions trip to Singapore. In the midst of that journey, God spoke to me and handed me an ultimatum for my life. With much pain, difficult decisions, and a farewell to a full scholarship, I submitted to God. Then, somehow I became a pastor's wife at the age of twenty. We had been married for only three and a half months, and to say I was not ready for ministry is the biggest understatement of the universe.

The startling Wednesday night, when we met at the church for the presbyter to inform the two men who made up the church that we were the new pastors, was an evening I shall not soon forget. The presbyter made a few opening comments and then said, "Brother Hughes, come and greet everyone."

Granted, everyone was me, one man, and the presbyter—a whopping total of three humans. All my new husband could think to say was "Let's all find a place to pray."

Accordingly, I knelt at that scratchy, splintery, old wooden pew that smelled like centuries-old varnish. As my head lay against the back of the bench, I cried and cried. I thought, *What are we doing here? I cannot do this! Surely they know that!* Panicked is a fitting word to describe my feelings that night.

Of course, I kept all this raging storm on the inside so that no one would know I was this afraid. I lived terrified that someone would realize I had no business being a pastor's wife because I had no idea how to pray or read my Bible. The imposter syndrome wasn't a thing back then, but I am sure I had it. And I had it bad. Laughingly, I comforted myself that at least I knew the books of the Bible, thanks to years of growing up with Bible verse sword drills on Wednesday nights. Truly, that was almost all I did know about my Bible unless being able to name several Bible characters and stories counted.

All of this set me on a path that I would not wish anyone else ever to travel. My situation brought to the surface everything from which I had been running for a long time. I was finally in the place the Lord had delivered me to although I couldn't possibly see it at the time.

During this time, my extended family was in turmoil. Due to some seemingly irreparable bad feelings and hurtful, divisive actions from a power struggle in court between my younger sister and my parents, my sister had fled Oklahoma to parts unknown. Even though she and I were not close, this was extremely dramatic and hurtful. Now I realize that I was not processing my feelings correctly at all. If I had been more emotionally and spiritually healthy, perhaps I could have worked to mitigate the family drama. Unfortunately, I was in survival mode and struggled to take care of myself.

Life was tough since we had moved several times. By then, I had restarted my college career at least twice, only to be forced to drop out again. I worked as a paraprofessional for a wonderful organization that endeavored to educate developmentally delayed students. My husband had a minimum-wage job, pushing shopping carts at a grocery store, as well as pastoring the barely surviving church we had just been assigned by the district superintendent. In the early days of our marriage, he had held a wonderful job as a policy editor at a large bank in the capital city of our state, but suddenly, we struggled to make ends meet each month while working every day and remodeling the church building every night.

While our tasks pushed us to mere survival on many fronts, the main battleground was my mind. To survive, I learned to stay busy. I must remain so busy that my mind had no choice but to acquiesce to the busyness and the schedule and did not have time for all the games and schemes I had skillfully concocted.

Shauna Niequist perfectly expresses how I felt during that time:

I feel like I am driving a car 100 miles an hour with music blaring out of open windows. I screech into a parking lot, throw the car in park, sprint into 7-11, and race to the back of the store. I throw my head under the Slurpee machine, and I fill my mouth with red Slurpee, tons and tons, running down my face and neck. I just keep gulping and gulping, sticky red corn syrup-y sludge, more and more, until I stand up, smeared and dripping, and race back to the car, on to the next thing, jamming the car into reverse, music at mind-numbing volume. That's how I feel. And what I want is a strawberry. I want one real strawberry. And I don't know how to get there.[22]

I knew I was running full speed ahead to destruction, but I had no clue of how to stop or how to do a hard reset. Instead, I just kept going, faster and faster.

To make matters worse, my husband had also been elected as a sectional youth leader in our state before we were married. The new responsibility led to many more complications with my identity and self-worth. I have distinct memories of attending youth committee meetings and truly believing that everyone there was more spiritual, more beautiful, more everything than I. Since I never felt like I fit, I knew when they found out what I really was, not only would they be disappointed but, sadly, my husband would lose his highly esteemed position. Surely, we would be ruined and exiled from ministry for a lifetime of misery. I lived—or pitifully existed—like this for years.

I would attend church services and hear the preacher talk about the love of God. All the while, I would sit in silence with the mind-numbing knowledge that God did not love me nor ever had because of all I had done or had not done to gain His love and approval. The love of God was a foreign concept to me as I never felt God's love and never thought it would be accessible for me.

I had grown up in church settings with authoritarian-type leaders who did not appear to demonstrate much love. The resulting ultra-conservative environment was all about looking perfectly holy on the outside, but not much was ever taught about character and the necessity of inward holiness. In this environment, incongruence abounded with the people I looked to as leaders and peers in the church.

Note: If you are in an environment where people aren't who they say they are, please pray very sincerely and ask God what you should do. A huge difference separates a church culture that is unhealthy, toxic, and performance-driven and a healthy church culture flowing from a God-based, truly biblical center. Leaders within a scriptural authority structure love people from hearts that have pure motives.

From this environment, I had deduced that God was probably always angry and upset with people like me. Presumably, He couldn't love me for a garden variety of reasons my mind would apply to any moment in time. Every time I turned around, I was in trouble with either the church leadership at every level or my family.

As a young teenager, I was even stopped by camp security on my way to a night service at a youth camp. Due to some circumstances that happened in my family's car on the drive to the campground, I was asked to sit in a room without the support of friends or family for hours while I was interrogated on and off for at least five hours. Only the mercy of the district superintendent who intervened that night saved me. However, when I was taken off the campground by my very angry father, I proclaimed to myself that I would never step foot on those grounds again.

Obviously, I was an expert in sin management at this point in my life. All I could do was manage my sin since I truly never believed I was worthy to be forgiven of my sin by God.

61

When the church falls prey to sin management, we usually resort to telling people moralisms. "Just stop that." "Get accountability." "Pray more and read your Bible." "Memorize scripture." Don't get me wrong, none of this activity is necessarily bad. Some of these things are even vital to our spiritual development. But there is something more that needs to be done to address the real disease.[23]

Living in this diseased state of sin management for years had taken a giant toll on my spirit, soul, and body.

Right now, some of you are reading this and concluding, *My goodness, she needed to get a grip and "pray through" or something!* However, others of you know exactly what I am talking about because you also have lived with this intense mind struggle so long that you don't even know what is normal. To live with a mind free from constant self-hate and self-condemnation is as strange a concept as your writing an essay in Mandarin Chinese. To live with joy and to feel the affirmation of the God we serve seem a pipe dream.

The other thing some of you think right now is: *Why didn't you get help?* Help in those days was costly. I don't mean monetary price. We were isolated and lived at least one hundred miles from almost everyone, so fellowship only occurred on Friday nights at sectional services. I am sure everyone on the outside looking in on us had the sense that we were fine. We were rebuilding a church that had been on the brink of closure, and it appeared that no one really worried about us much. Since I had been mostly backslidden in the years just prior to pastoring, I didn't have church friends.

The main objective in my daily life was carefully maintaining the veneer that made everyone think I was okay and not in need of anything. When one is living with the life-draining imposter syndrome and endless perfectionism, every outside conversation has the potential to expose one's inner life. Since I had no desire to reveal who I really was, authentic conversation was out of the question!

Eventually, I accomplished my goal of a bachelor's degree in elementary education and became an elementary teacher. Our son was born a few years later. One would think that things would be easier by now, but the weight of the self-hate and even heavier self-inflicted grudge against myself had become even harder to manage. They had increased and required much more space in my mind.

As a teacher, one way I coped with the mind battle was to throw myself into the teaching profession. I worked early mornings and late nights in my classroom. I constantly read professional books to better myself because a harmful pattern had begun to emerge in my life. If I could control my environment, no one would ever know I was in shambles on the inside. If I could appear as if everything was perfect and in finely tuned working order, no one would know that I was a complete inner wreck.

I learned that if I behaved as a control freak, people would not want to get too close because I was a hard person to deal with and impossible to please with anything. I second-guessed every decision from myself and those around me. I redid, reworked, and finessed stuff continually—both mine and everyone else's. This would be how I coped for the next ten or fifteen years at school, home, and church.

Side note: To everyone from Victory Worship Center in those years, please accept my sincerest apology for living this way, in a fog most days. I have already apologized to most of the wonderful people in that church, but if I have missed anyone, please know that I really did love you and cared for you as best as I could at that moment.

Regarding the family drama, around 2007 or so, I made a trip to the state where my sister lived. I had prayed repeatedly and asked the Lord to help me reconcile with my sister. I was feeling bereft that I had a sister about whom I didn't know much. This was such a painful time for all of us. Looking back, I was being forced to learn and practice many things like grace, unconditional forgiveness, and true love for my sister while letting go of the painful past. Obviously, we were both working through shame and guilt, and those seeds bore fruit in the most undesirable ways. While the trip was tough on many fronts, it did begin to open the door slightly for a true relationship.

I have asked my sister to write a memory for this book. I insert her story here as her recollection will help to illustrate how shame keeps us bound and unable to do what we know is right for the moment. When I read this story for the first time, I was taken aback by the flood of painful memories and tears that accompanied this story.

This was around 2003 or 2004. One Christmas I bought gifts for little Blakers, my nephew. It was a truck, a cool game, and a silly toy. I wrapped them all up in excitement. But when I went to get them bundled for shipping, I couldn't move forward. I started wondering why I had the right to send him gifts. We weren't close. I wasn't really part of the family at that time, and I had lingering shame from all of the events that had come before. So the gifts sat there. Christmas kept getting closer and closer, and I didn't have the tools to deal with all the emotions I was feeling. So I moved the gifts to a coat closet. It became such an emotional barrier that Christmas came and went, and the gifts remained in the closet. I felt really stupid by this point because it seemed so easy just to get a few gifts and send them for Christmas. It turned out to be impossible for my developmental progress at that point.

The gifts stayed in the closet until the summer of the next year. I thought it was stupid to leave them in the closet. I finally pulled them out and unwrapped them. There they sat, vicious reminders of how I didn't feel like a part of my family and couldn't get around all of the emotions that sending gifts invoked. I ended up donating them that summer.

Christmas came around again, and there I went. I bought more gifts that next year and was determined to send them. I wrapped them, trying to move past the previous year's defeat. The same barriers came up again: shame, fear of rejection, embarrassment, and dread. This time I just took the gifts and gave them to some neighborhood kids. After that, I didn't try to buy any more gifts. I accepted total defeat. This stirred a deep guilt. Blake was innocent in all of this, and I really wanted to give him gifts. But due to my own internal shame and fear, I couldn't overcome all that had come before Blake.

By the time I had worked through my internal shame and fear, Blake had grown up. —VeAna Archer

Somewhere around 2010, my husband was out of town for the week on a mission trip to Guatemala, and I decided to watch some YouTube videos about a subject I had heard people discussing. Of course, I didn't think I had shame issues, but for good measure, I would watch a couple of the videos. I told myself I was only watching to see if the videos would be a help to any of those people we were discipling and teaching Bible studies. My perfect plan was to watch one YouTube video each evening that week.

At first, I was completely angry at the minister in the videos. I thought, *Who is he to tell me how I feel? He is just so arrogant!*

I raged and railed mentally but nonetheless could feel the truth coming dangerously close to my tightly held, perfectly constructed persona and carefully controlled behaviors. As I worked through the videos, the realization hit me like five tons of bricks! *Shame is a thing, and I think I have it.*

Shame was my issue? All the signs pointed straight to shame, yet I had trouble believing this. For years, I had taught Bible studies to people and told them that God loved them and cared for them. All the while I was not able to believe this amazing truth truly for myself. At this point, you're welcome to send this book flying into the nearest trash can, but if you do that, you might still be stuck in the swamp where you are right now.

Just take a break. Take a walk, a chocolate or a coffee break. Come back when you're ready. We will be here awaiting your return.

What Is Shame?

I had to come to the painful truth that I had not been able to receive the love of God because I had a grudge against myself. I wasn't angry at God. I was extremely angry and filled with rage at myself.

According to Chester Wright, who wrote a revelatory scriptural and investigative dive on shame that I referenced in the introduction,

"The Greek word for shame is *intrope*. *Intrope* means spiritual confusion or paralysis."[24]

For an entire lifetime, I had lived in perpetual spiritual confusion or paralysis! Even as the wife of a pastor and district official, leading and teaching others, I was spiritually confused and yet had no idea.

Shame Defined

Shame is sometimes referred to as a painful emotion caused by a strong sense of guilt, embarrassment, unworthiness, or disgrace.[25] Shame is also defined as humiliation and feeling embarrassed from inadequacy or inferiority. But the most concerning definition is that shame is the ultimate result of losing respect for yourself.

> Shame is never harmless, inconsequential, or easily ignored. It will not go away of its own accord. The person with shame will never outgrow it. Attempting to bury it in the subconscious mind only makes it more dangerous, destructive, debilitating, and insidious. And, finally, it only breeds more and more shame until it produces total spiritual paralysis. Eventually, it either destroys the affected person and their world or they finally get desperate enough to seek God's help.[26]

So many times, shame is something we cannot verbalize, explain, quantify, or fully comprehend. Brown says, "If you can't measure it, it doesn't exist." Shame is insidious in its complete annihilation of our souls and bodies. By the time we realize something is terribly wrong, it has the tightest grip on our minds and refuses to let go no matter how much we beg, pull, and tug.

A verse in James still brings chills to my entire being. The entire third chapter of James is marvelous, but the following verses pack a hefty punch.

> *But if you have bitter envy and self-seeking in your hearts, do not boast and lie against the truth. This wisdom does not descend from above but*

is earthly, sensual, and demonic. For where envy and self-seeking exist, confusion and every evil thing are there. But the wisdom that is from above is first pure, then peaceable, gentle, willing to yield, full of mercy and good fruits, without partiality and without hypocrisy (James 3:14-17, NKJV).

This passage illustrates wholly what I have tried to say through the past few pages. As a survival technique against revealing who I was on the inside, I fulfilled this verse! I was self-seeking, constantly comparing myself with everyone else, and had loads of confusion. As a result, I had unwittingly created a ringside seat for the enemy of my soul.

This doesn't mean that I was possessed of devils by any means. I didn't even realize that I had given in to earthly wisdom in the form of the swamp and all of its slimy creatures: inconsistency, pride, fleshly behavior, approval addiction, imposter syndrome, passive aggression, perfectionism, anger, control of everyone around me, and a crippling failure to be able to recognize or receive God's love for myself and everyone else.[27]

I want to make a crucial point that toxic thinking and shame will eventually lead every human down a road of misery and pharisaical behaviors. Everything I hated in people as I grew up in the church, I had allowed to become rooted in myself. I just held the grudge and self-hate against myself so long that I developed distrust and bitterness against everyone I knew.

Shame tells us that we are mistakes, impossibly flawed individuals, and failures. Shame tells us we will never measure up. It threatens that the worst thing that can happen is when people find out who we are and thus reject us. "When your foundation is threatened, your mind will start racing: your soul will feel the internal quaking that results from a life constructed on a lie."[28] I have manifested this quite true statement. In many instances, I realized I was angry. Self-hate was building in my human spirit, but I would just double down and spew the venom that anger and hate produce.

Shame has a way of forcing lives to perform exactly like a roller coaster. Shame causes people to be inconsistent in their relationships with God and all others. Bishop Wright says that unresolved shame is the most debilitating spiritual condition the church contends with, and it is the foundational reason for almost all backsliding. He goes on to say that shame causes tremendous inconsistency in believers.

Some days I was up and most days I was down. I would try to be consistent in my prayer and Bible reading, but regardless of my extreme control of everything else in my life, my good intentions would slip. I would plummet back to the normal, crazy cycle. Over the years, I have lost more Bible reading charts than is even possible in a lifetime. I have spent thousands of dollars on notebooks, Bibles, pens, devotions, and journals, desperately searching for a system that would work for me. I have countless planners, binders, and all sorts of products designed to organize my inner life, in vain. Of course, this only led me deeper into the swamp of self-hate and misery.

Things We Don't Understand about Shame

In Joel 2:25-28, shame is removed before the promise of the outpouring of the Spirit arrives. All my life I have heard about the great end-time revival. I know it is the will of God for billions to come to a revelation of the mighty God in Christ and to be water baptized in the name of Jesus before the second coming of Christ. However, too much of the church as a whole is stuck in the swamp of shame, teetering on a faulty foundation of the Word of God. Precious people go to church each week and hear inspirational sermons and life-changing messages. There is only one problem—lives remain unchanged, and the world continues its march into the dark depths of hell.

Why? One word: shame.

Most of the church world doesn't understand shame. If someone mentioned shame, they would say, "Oh, we don't have shame. People just need to _____" (insert any word or phrase here). Here are fill-in-the-blank terms I have heard:

✦ Pray through.
✦ Get over it.

+ Move on; it's past stuff.
+ Quit being so emotional.
+ Realize the Holy Ghost will fix everything.
+ Pray or read the Bible more.

As we have traveled from church to church most weekends, I have helplessly watched good folks not respond to the preached Word of God and simply ignore the moving of God's Spirit. On one occasion, the pastor asked me what I thought was happening among the people during the altar service.

Very carefully, I ventured onto the deserted island of boldness and with a stuttering hesitation responded, "It's shame. They want to believe the message, but they cannot believe they are the ones to do XYZ from the message because they have a faulty foundation of self that doesn't come from God's Word."

When I said this, I was trying to say that people with shame hear the Word preached but cannot apply it to their lives. The faulty lies their minds and spirits have believed for so long say, "Not you, not here, not ever because you are flawed. You are no good. God uses everyone else but not you because of whachamacallit, which happened years ago. You are never going to work in your area of gifting, so just forget it." So people do.

"Shame issues lead to emotional and spiritual deadness where people isolate and withdraw eventually."[29] People with shame issues really wish they could activate their giftings, their calling, and their burdens, but when they try, their feet are firmly mired in the swampland of the soul. They finally give in and think, *Ah, maybe the next revival I will be better. I will try again next year after camp season.*

If this is you, you are not flawed! You are created in the image of God. God knows your name and has an exact count of the number of hairs on your sweet head! You are not a flawed individual—you need the awareness and revelation that God is giving right now to help you escape the pull of the boggy mud of shame's faulty foundation.

We sometimes tell people with shame, "You just need healthy self-esteem." I have heard this so many times it makes me want to use that

69

little green emoji for "word vomit" here! Where do people obtain a healthy self-esteem? Where does self-esteem come from? That thinking is flawed and will forever be faulty simply because it is not based on the eternally true Word of God.

We fall prey to humanistic philosophy when we think we can possibly make ourselves better merely by viewing ourselves as better, happier, the next versions of our best selves, or highly esteemed. Our worth and our view of ourselves will always come directly from Scripture and God's Spirit. When we realize who we are in Christ and what He has ordained for us to do in His really big kingdom, we will perceive ourselves properly.

Wright says, "Esteem for myself cannot come from me. Accepting my worth also cannot come from myself." This is why telling someone to feel better about himself or herself does not help anyone. This is also why reading more books and watching more YouTube videos and Instagram reels about improving your self-esteem don't help; rather, that only makes things worse.

Shame leads people to feel inferior and insufficient, not ever adequate. They have trouble receiving a compliment and never think they are capable of launching their God call and gift. Shame blocks them from receiving love and the affirmation they desperately seek. Shame leads us to numb ourselves and our feelings. The only problem with numbing is that when we numb the stuff that hurts, we also numb the stuff that feels good.

Again, this book is not intended to be medical advice, but this also happens when people take mood/emotional medicine to stabilize them. They cannot feel the painful stuff, but they also cannot feel the positive feelings. The scope includes God's presence as that provides a good and positive feeling.

"Shame is a sickness of the soul. Most poignant experience of the self by the self, whether felt in humiliation or cowardice or in a sense of failure to cope successfully with a change. Shame is a wound felt from the inside—dividing us both from ourselves and each other."[30]

When we have shame, we are basically spiritually paralyzed. Shame is the biggest reason that people don't pray. When we don't respect ourselves, how would it be possible to pray with faith that God will answer any of our prayers? If I continually keep a grudge against myself, how can I be open and honest with God?

Chester Wright speaks of people living in torment because they cannot figure out why they're the way they are and cannot seem to do anything to make themselves better. This is an explanation for shame. When I cannot see myself or others clearly, I am warped. My perceptions, my thoughts, and my assumptions are a mess, and I cannot see anything the right way. This pathway will usually lead to bitterness and a lack of forgiveness. As we've covered previously, this is a self-made prison that is almost impossible to escape on our own.

Revelation of Loving Ourselves

As we mentioned in the preceding principle, the love we have for ourselves is the key to healing from shame. In Mark 12:28-31, we know that God has commanded us to love Him and then to love our neighbor as ourselves. This sounds great. We can quote it and preach about it, but we cannot seem to really comprehend what this means.

> Mark 12:28-31 defines the three fundamental relationships in our lives: God—Others—Myself. The pivotal relationship here is this: It's how I feel about myself, and if I cannot love myself, that will impact every other relationship—including God. I am not lovable simply because I don't love myself. God loves us because of who we are—not because of what we do. God commands us to love Him and each other as we love our own self. If we cannot love ourselves, how can we receive God's love and love from our brothers and sisters?[31]

When we don't feel love or we don't obey God's Word, we hide in guilt. Guilt and shame always make us hide. In hiding, we cannot get the help we direly need.

This was a huge key revelation for me as I went forward in my healing. I realized that God had always loved me but that I had built

71

my life on the faulty foundation that God didn't love me due to my inadequacies and my double life as a teen. It has taken me years to be able to receive the love of God and the love of others through my close relationships with friends and the family of God. "The soul needs love as vitally as the lungs need oxygen; without it, the soul dies, just as the body does without oxygen."[32] Boom!

Right here we see the tendency to slide back into the swamp and to tell ourselves to be something we're not! Please remember that feelings do not have to be true to be real. The feelings you have right now might not be accurate. In later chapters, we will talk more about a revelation of the love of God and His atoning power.

Symptoms of Shame

We often confuse shame and guilt as we fight our way through the swampland of the soul. Guilt tells us we have done wrong. Shame tells us that we are wrong.

> This is a key symptom of shame. Other emotional symptoms of shame: inferiority, depression, extreme fear of embarrassment, humiliation, hopelessness, loneliness, helplessness, feeling flawed or damaged, extreme guilt over opportunities, dreams, hopes, plans, etc., regret with deep sorrow, alienation or abandonment, abiding anger with a quick temper—make them pay, unexplainable fear or terror, fear of failure or rejection, shyness or fear of meeting people, feelings of confusion, paralysis over decisions to the extreme, absence of peace or joy in daily life, distrustful of everyone, blame and intense self-blame, feeling unlovable or unwanted like an outsider, feelings of never good enough, inability or unwillingness to forgive others, negative self-talk, judgmentalism, uselessness, control, obsession with perfection, fear of mistakes, superiority or arrogance, defeatism, worthlessness, the feeling of "I just can't do anything right," self-blame, self-hatred, desire to punish or harm oneself, and suicidal feelings.[33]

72

Perfectionism and control are two of the strongest indicators of shame. Many will not agree with me here, but I have come to the painful conclusion that both control and perfectionism behaviors are shields we wield to keep people at arm's length, distant from knowledge of the real us. Reimer says that shields are dangerous because they are indiscriminate. They not only block out the painful things, but the shields also block the very God who is trying to heal us.

Brené Brown speaks of a shield that we struggle to carry around because when we have shame, we must keep our real selves hidden at all costs. She asserts:

> Perfectionism is a twenty-ton shield that we lug around thinking it will protect us when, in fact, it's the thing that's really preventing us from taking flight. Perfectionism is, at its core, all about trying to earn approval and acceptance. Perfectionism is addictive because when we invariably do experience shame, judgment, and blame, we often believe it's because we weren't perfect enough. So we become even more entrenched in our quest to live, look, and do everything just right. This never happens in a vacuum. It touches everyone around us. It's suffocating to our families and friends.[34]

One can never approach close enough to see behind the proverbial curtain of the Wizard of Oz.

Again, *Soul Care* speaks to this issue in our hearts:

> You are only as sick as the secrets you keep. If you are going to walk free, you must not walk in secrecy. It is a powerful thing to be open and honest. There is no healing where there is pretending. . . . We need to lay down our defensive shields that are attempts at self-protection and begin to establish some healthy boundaries for ourselves.[35]

In his syllabus for his seminar on shame, Chester Wright quotes James Gilligan:

Shame deadens the feelings of being human, and leads to rage. The sources of love for the self are love from others and one's own love for oneself. Children who fail to receive sufficient love from others fail to build up reserves of self-love, and the capacity for self-love, which enables them to survive the inevitable rejections and humiliations that even the most fortunate of people cannot avoid. Without feelings of love, the self feels numb, empty, and dead. To be overwhelmed by shame and humiliation causes the destruction of self-esteem. Without a certain amount of self-esteem, the self collapses and the soul dies.

But a joyless life is a synonym for hell. A man who does not love and cannot love is, in effect, condemned to hell. His entire environment, from which—without love—he is cut off, is without enjoyment for him, and thus the world he "lives" in is a source of emptiness and emotional suffocation for him. Both the world and the self are experienced and perceived emotionally as being dead, inanimate, without a soul—without feelings.

Since the sense of aliveness and humanness that comes from loving includes a vulnerability to pain, only those who are capable of risking pain can experience joy. Emotional health is not the absence of pain. It is the capacity to bear painful feelings when they occur, without letting them stop us from loving others and continuing to feel worthy of love ourselves. A person can expose himself to the vulnerability of loving another person only if he has enough self-esteem to protect himself from the devastation he would suffer if that love were not reciprocated. He cannot afford to give to another the love which he cannot give himself. If he has taken the chance and lost, the results can be immediately and devastatingly lethal, to others and to himself. Without love (by which I mean here love for oneself), the self collapses, the soul dies, and the psyche goes to hell. Men will quickly and ferociously attack others, even kill them, if they think it will

74

prevent their own souls from being murdered. What they immediately discover when they commit a violent act, however, is that this strategy is self-defeating. And that is why so many murderers finally decide to end their own lives as well.

In other words, to love something or someone is to enjoy it, or him, or her. Where there is joy, there is love. Conversely, where there is no love, there is no joy. . . . And the cause of lovelessness (the incapacity for love) is joylessness (the incapacity for joy); and vice versa. The chief causes of the incapacity for love and joy are shame (the lack of self-love, which inhibits love of others, and stimulates hatred toward them, and fear of them, instead); and guilt (the presence of self-hate, which inhibits self-love, and stimulates fear and condemnation of one's own hostile and destructive impulses and wishes).

Among the clinical and behavioral syndromes caused by shame are paranoia, narcissism, sociopathy, selfishness, sadism, and revenge; whereas guilt causes, among other things, depression, penance, self-punishment, self-sacrifice, martyrdom, and masochism.[36]

I want you to stop and reread that last, long sentence. The progression of shame, without proper healing and attention, leads to paranoia, sadism, and sociopathy. This is crazy stuff!

We really must realize how powerful shame is. When we comprehend the danger, we must attempt to stop the progression in so many of the people we love, including loving ourselves enough to begin the road of healing from shame.

You are worth the struggle!

Sources of Shame

Wright says the primary sources of shame are:

✦ My own actions—things I did that I wish I had not done.
✦ Or those things that I did not do that I wish I had done.

75

- ✦ Sins I committed that were damaging to me or someone else that I cannot seem to get over or forget about like fornication, adultery, homosexuality, or pornography.
- ✦ Rejection.
- ✦ Alienation or emotional abandonment from trauma, sickness, divorce, infidelity, suicide, and so on.
- ✦ Abuse: physical or sexual from others, or self-inflicted pain.
- ✦ Class rejection: a group of people as a result of persecution, enslavement, defeat in war, cast out of a group.
- ✦ Self-destructive behavior: shame is the root cause of all self-destructive behavior whether that be physical, eating disorders, mental, or anything in that category.

Abuse of any Sort

I feel to take this moment to discuss abuse frankly. I am quite aware that some of you reading this book have been the victims of abuse. In the first chapter, I stated that this book is not meant to dispense counseling or medical advice. However, if you have been a victim of abuse or have a close family member or friend who has been a victim, please know that you are seen and heard. Know that the Lord still loves you so very much. The Lord still fights for you even if you cannot sense Him near you. If you were abused in any way and have kept that a secret, please seek the help you need to move forward, whether that be a spiritual authority, therapist, or close confidant. Secrets tend to grow into malicious wounds in the dark.

Abuse of any sort is wrong. God considers abuse evil and detestable, as well as those who cover it up. (See Psalm 11:5; Deuteronomy 22:25-27; Romans 1:18 [NLT]; II Samuel 22:28; Luke 4:18-19.) Secrets keep hidden shame and evil things in the darkness.

Shame sometimes keeps us cloaked in silence for wrongs done to us or to others. Perpetrators may try to manipulate the victims into silence through threats of hurting their loved ones or through gaslighting and trying to make the survivor think the abuse was his or her fault. That is a devious trick. Secrets only allow the perpetrator space to continue to inflict more abuse on others and keep the survivor from healing. Speaking up and bringing the abuse to light is a huge step toward healing, whether for yourself or to advise others who have been abused.

Abuse is not only physical. Abuse takes on multiple forms such as physical abuse or violence; sexual abuse; emotional/verbal abuse; financial abuse; psychological abuse; and cultural abuse. Abuse can be incredibly traumatic. A survivor is not responsible for the behavior of an abuser.[37]

Spiritual Abuse

Spiritual hurt is a reality. Dr. David Bernard has a podcast on YouTube, entitled "What is Spiritual Abuse? Episode 97." Therein, he speaks of spiritual abuse and hurt. This term wasn't even known a few years ago, but now, we must discuss this. I will share several of his points, but do yourself a favor and locate this episode so you can hear him make these points.

A spiritual authority that is biblical and correct will not be abusive. Only God has absolute authority, not man. The number one sign that a leader is headed for trouble is if he thinks he has absolute authority and doesn't have accountability. When this happens, he becomes a lord over God's flock. In I Peter 5:1-4, we hear a warning to overseers. Overseers are not to cheat people, deceive people, take money inappropriately, seek dishonest gain, or act like a dictator, which is acting like an authoritarian.

Power must come from the Spirit of God and not from carnal or fleshly means like coercion, browbeating, or exploiting people. If overseers have the wrong motive for serving the flock, they will become prideful and egotistical and have the propensity to enact physical, emotional, or even sexual abuse, using a false rationale that they are above the law. If any of these things happen in a local assembly, the people have a right to speak up and contact their spiritual authorities, [or in the worst case, local authorities such as law enforcement or health services] in the chain of authority above the overseer.

Abuse is not to happen in the name of religion for any reason or situation. If this has happened to you, you might be feeling false shame. This means that you feel shame of something that happened that is not your fault but is projected to you as if it's your fault. Seek counsel. Follow your chain of authority and report any overseers who are excessive in their handling of the flock of God.

Shame begets shame. The more shame I feel, the more shame I hold. Shame is very cyclical. One emotion or toxic thought leads to another. Soon, the mind is trapped in the vortex of severely damaging emotions. The cycle of shame finally convinces you, "I am so flawed that there is no power to change me." Then, distorted thinking begins to warp all your decision making and daily processing. The worldly wisdom of James 3 eventually overtakes you, leading to envy and self-seeking, which take you along the pathway identified earlier.

In the book *The Gifts of Imperfection*, Brené Brown states:

> According to Dr. Hartling, in order to deal with shame, some of us move away by withdrawing, hiding, silencing ourselves, and keeping secrets. Some of us move toward by seeking to appease and please. And some of us move against by trying to gain power over others, by being aggressive, and by using shame to fight shame (like sending mean emails)[38]

[or posting all of our garbage online and getting 38,998 opinions of how to "fix" our problems without going to God for ourselves].

Yes, I am purposefully pounding you with hard-hitting quotes because I understand and realize how pervasive that shame is and how deeply rooted our behaviors are. I just know in the Holy Ghost that a few of you are yearning with every fiber of your being to be free of the shame that has taken you captive against your will.

Getting out of the Cycle of Shame

Shame is a primitive human emotion that most of us have faced at one time or another. The problem is that we are terrified to speak of shame or to discuss it. As we have already said, the less we speak of something, the more control it has over us.

We must begin to recognize shame and move through the feelings of insignificance and unworthiness while allowing ourselves to progress through and out of the swamp. We have to talk about why our shame has us so bound, and we must move into authenticity with each other. How do we progress with this?

When we have shame, we fear we are so unlovable and flawed that nothing—and surely not God—could ever fix us. When we live with shame, we have likely persuaded ourselves that our stories are never to be told. We would die of embarrassment if someone uncovered the real back story of our lives! Shame is all about fear, according to Brené Brown. This is crazy because as believers and students of the Word of God, we know that fear is not good.

We oftentimes quote II Timothy 1:7, claiming that there is no fear in love and that we are to have a sound mind with self-control. We are really great at quoting this all the while maintaining our pious perfection and eyebrow-lifted smug spiritual arrogance. When we demonstrate perfectionism, shame is always present.

But the real question is: How does a person get to an absence of fear, a sound mind, and self-control? It sounds like an amazing

> Shame is the birthplace of perfectionism. —Brené Brown.

concoction Willy Wonka produces at the chocolate factory but surely not something we could enjoy on a daily, minute-by-minute basis!

We must work to understand shame and to realize that this issue hides in every one of our swamps of appearance, body image, family, parenting, money, work, health, addiction, aging, marriage, relationships, and religion.[39] Each of us has countless hurts, hangups, and a long history of regrets at least two miles long. Some of us have heartbreaking trauma, and our struggles have been real. Really real.

We could replay comments from parents, teachers, spiritual leaders, family members, spouses, siblings, and friends. We could tell you about times of darkness and depression so deep that we thought we would never escape it. Some have had chronic sickness and a myriad of physical symptoms that make no sense. We must realize that the less we talk about shame, the more shame we have. Shame must have these three things to usurp the control over our lives: secrecy, silence, and judgment.

To escape the clutches of shame, we must begin to identify the sources of shame, and we must recognize the messages we are telling ourselves about our stories of shame. We must reach out and begin sharing stories with the people we know we can trust and thus build authenticity around us. This in itself will begin to tear at the barriers of silent, hidden rules and assumptions that we hold near and dear.

Hannah Brencher has a phrase, "Thank your limp!" I love this. She draws this phrase from the Old Testament and Jacob's wrestling match with the angel. At daybreak, the angel touched Jacob's hip, and he would forever limp. But through that moment, Jacob received a name change that would change the direction of his life. The limp was revealing to Jacob as he saw God face to face, but he had a story for the remainder of his life.

Hannah speaks of depression as her limp, but she says that her limp gives people hope not to discount the battle to get to the limp. When we allow people into our mess, transformation will take place, and we will receive something better.

> When you talk about your limp, something cool usually happens. People get more honest. They open up about their own hard stuff. We learn to rally with one another and not be defined by our weaknesses. Our weaknesses become a bridge instead of a roadblock. We become little light holders on that bridge, helping other people find their way out of the dark. It's beautiful to be a light to someone else. We get the chance every day, even if we don't see it. But light is only powerful because it has known the darkness before.[40]

Reimer declares, "In true community, people live open, honest, and confessional lives in a culture of grace. There is no hiding or pretending. Secrets are toxic to the well-being of the soul. If you are going to experience a breakthrough, then you must resolve to live confessional lives with no secrets."

Can we just be honest here? Hmmm, the irony of that statement. When we think of our places of worship and our circles of friends, can we truly say that those are cultures of grace? If not, why not? Are we surrounding ourselves with people who truly want the best for us, which includes healing from shame and toxic thinking?

Please take some time to pray about this concept of churches and circles of friends. I am not telling you to change churches or to replace all of your friends. What I am encouraging you to do is to take a long, hard look at those with whom you fellowship on a regular basis, the people who sit at your life table, who influence your inner self more than most. Does your local church encourage authentic relationships with each other and with God? Is it a biblically based church that believes in inner healing through the Word of God and the working of the Holy Spirit? Does it not merely slap a defective label on bad people and move on as if nothing happened?

When we are able to identify the causes of shame, we will begin the journey out of the swamp and realize that healing is accessible for each of us. Honesty, vulnerability, and openness lead to healed souls, which in turn allows us to be connected to God in a way we never thought possible. But the cycle continues. Our relationships will begin to be so improved that we will wish we had worked through this earlier in life and not stayed mired in the swamp so long.

When we finally own our stories, we will move toward authenticity and embrace vulnerability. I know, that sounds scary right now, but I promise it's the only way out of the swamp. You can make an exit from life on the inconsistent roller coaster.

As Zach Williams reminds in his song, "No Longer Slaves," we receive freedom from fear with our entry into the family of God and our recognition of our rightful place there.

Keep fighting for one more chapter, my friend!

Reflection

1. List the shame behaviors you have seen in yourself recently or in the past. Be honest with yourself here.
2. What parts of your life are like a roller coaster?
3. What sources of shame are in your past?
4. Have you allowed yourself to be open to your friend circle or community about those things, or are they cloaked in secrecy and darkness?
5. To whom will you open up about the dark places? Name someone here so you don't lose your resolve.
6. What are the places or areas where you have judged yourself too harshly?

Soundtracks to Save the Soul

Ministry keeps us on the road, in the car or airplane for long periods. As we travel, we have grown to love listening to podcasts and audiobooks. We endeavor to make the windshield time count.

Jon Acuff is one author we particularly enjoy. He is witty, relational, and easy to listen to as we drive. He makes us laugh but, at the same time, wrings us out of our toxic thinking with his intentional life messages. In one of his most recent books, *Soundtracks*, he describes something that all of us do on a minute-by-minute basis. We tell ourselves stories. Or, according to Acuff, we repeat the same soundtracks over and over. I want you to read his book, so I will not go into many details here except to give a few choice morsels.

Jon Acuff claims, "Overthinking is when what you think gets in the way of what you want." This statement explains shame in such a concise way! Minds lost in the swamp of shame are minds that are so busy they can hardly see their way clear to the next stop sign. Most people with shame spend so much valuable time overthinking every decision and each detail that they are exhausted before they ever make it out of bed in the morning.

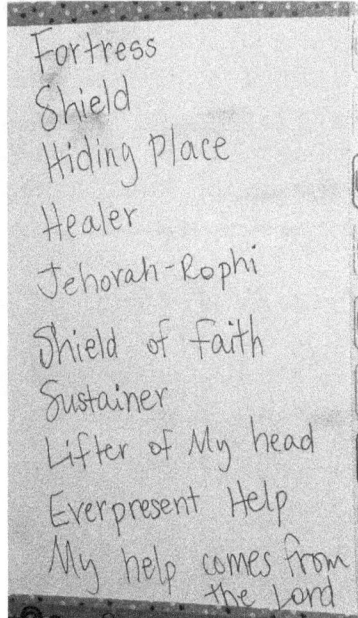

Fortress
Shield
Hiding Place
Healer
Jehovah-Rophi
Shield of faith
Sustainer
Lifter of My head
Everpresent Help
My help comes from the Lord

Acuff figured out that thoughts played long enough eventually become our personal soundtracks. These soundtracks play every waking moment and, as we will discover, continue to roll even while we sleep. Jon added a quote by a retired Navy SEAL, David Goggins. "The most important conversations you will ever have are the ones you have with yourself. You wake up with them, you walk around with them, you go to bed with them and eventually, you learn to act on them. Whether they be good or bad."

In other words: soundtracks. If your thoughts are good and not toxic, they help propel you through each day with encouragement and happiness. In that case, you have fantastic soundtracks that play in your mind. Go ahead, skip to the corner of the game, and collect two hundred dollars as you grab a coffee.

But if you have soundtracks that are remotely controlled from the swamp, you already know. Yep! Those thoughts will most likely be filled to the brim and overflowing with toxicity and badness. I am fairly sure that badness isn't a good word, but here, we need it. Some of our soundtracks are just plain bad and are in dire need of replacement. Unless our minds make the switch to a new tune, we might be free from jail or the swamp but still imprisoned by the shame vortex of the mind. A friend of ours called his overthinking and shame vortex "the mind monsters." So appropriate.

This begs the question: How do we change bad soundtracks?

First, a story about a girl and her record player.

One year for Christmas, I received a record player that was a white-hinged box with red and blue stripes and a long arm that held a tiny needle. Yes, back in the day we had record players that played black discs called records. Funny enough, they're back in vogue now, so perhaps you'll be familiar enough with this old-school concept.

I had some records that played my favorite songs. I would put a record on the turntable and watch it spin as I joyfully listened to the music. My little sister would hear the music, burst into my room, and insist on joining in the fun. What would usually happen is that her curiosity would get the better of her, and she would extend her little finger to feel the record spinning. You already know.

When her pudgy finger touched that record, one of two things would happen. Sometimes, both things happened, which was never good. One, the needle would be pushed out of its notch and would scratch. We would hear the awful noise indicating that my precious little record was scratched and would always re-re-re-re-re-re-repeat itself at that exact place. Two, that heavy touch would bounce the needle to a different track. The machine would switch to a different song but never to my favorite.

Either of these actions would rapidly advance us to the next frame of the story with the two sisters pulling hair and yelping at the tops of our lungs. Finally, Mom would come and beat us back into submission with a clothes hanger. Please do not call the Department of Human Services. We will not file charges, nor was any human seriously or permanently hurt by the above behavior remedy.

When we play soundtracks that are toxic, we tend to scratch every record in our brains. This happens in many different ways. For years, I constantly waited for the shoe to drop and for the horrible to happen. If I'm not mistaken, we refer to this as the worst-case scenario. If my husband told me he would arrive home by 11:30 PM from a long road trip, at precisely 11:32 PM, when he hadn't yet shown up, my ever-flawed and horribly scratched soundtrack would be on repeat. My mind would screech into high gear. Within nanoseconds, my husband had been in a horrible wreck and the highway patrol was on their way to my house. Sure they would give me the terrible news, I was planning the funeral, down to the color of the casket!

Not two minutes later, I imagined my life in ruins as I woefully contemplated my future without my husband. Often, I would almost be in tears at this point and walk to the bedroom to smell his pillow one more time, to remember what it meant to have him near. . . . My dear spouse would saunter through the door, thinking I was missing him so much I had a death grip on his pillow.

Asking for a friend, has this ever happened to you? Come on! If you lie, you fry! Just be honest and slightly nod your head in agreement that you know exactly what I mean by the doom and gloom, worst-case disaster scenarios in your mind.

Soundtracks are usually the biggest hurdle we face with shame. We have trained our minds so well that they are running to and fro at all times of the day and night, doing our bidding. As I have written this book, I have had to work hard to remember stories that aren't sad, bad, and terrible. It's been tough to recollect the positive things that have happened because for so long, I refused to allow myself to have fun, be happy, or even be content in the moment.

Jon Acuff refers to toxic thinking as broken soundtracks. These are the negative assessments you tell yourself about yourself and your world. I would guess that most of you reading this book are quite familiar with these broken soundtracks. These repetitive soundtracks have cost many of us too much time.

When I think back over the last twenty or so years, I have squandered time with the broken tracks in my mind. That wasted time will never be reclaimed, so I must work to redeem it through the words in this book.

Habits of Negativity

According to Jon Acuff, your brain builds on overthinking's habit of negativity by doing three additional things:

+ Lying about your memories,
+ Confusing fake trauma with real trauma, and
+ Believing what it already believes.

I don't think anyone intentionally lies about their memories. As we grow older, our memories change and details morph. I have learned to say that memory is a great betrayer.

While we're traveling, we often listen to Malcolm Gladwell's podcast, *Revisionist History*. He interviewed hordes of folks about the subject of memory for a podcast. Both Acuff and Gladwell report that certain memories create experiences we remember incorrectly.

If asked, we would most likely be able to remember certain tragic world events like the vehicle accident involving Princess Diana, the Challenger explosion, the worldwide COVID-19 pandemic shutdown, or the New York City events on 9/11. In Oklahoma, we sadly recall the bombing of the Alfred P. Murrah building. The interesting thing is that we remember those events differently based on our precise location, our mind-set at that time, or the way we framed those events according to our emotional health.

Our minds persist in soundtracks such as fear, rejection, and anger. When our soundtracks are broken or toxic or both, they grow in power each time we hear them played in our minds. Take fear for an example. My account about my husband's arrival five minutes late from a road trip demonstrates a pervasive, toxic soundtrack about fear. My mind immediately went to that toxic soundtrack before I could reframe or rethink. At the time, I wasn't sure how to rethink and thus get the broken record to change.

Dr. Caroline Leaf has conducted years of study about the brain and the mind. She has quite a bit to say about the misuse of our minds and what that produces. She explains, "If our minds are messed up, our lifestyles are messed up, and when our lifestyles are messed up, our mental and physical health suffers."[41]

While we understand that the Word of God has quite a bit to say about our minds and how they contribute to the spirit, soul, and body connection, we usually either do not realize the tremendous impact or simply choose to ignore the connection. "When the presence and power of God are part of our belief system, but absent from our practice, there are significant gaps in the integration of faith into our lives."[42] Again, incongruence leads to confusion and vice versa.

This takes us back to earlier chapters about knowing what we ought to do but not doing it, which allows for continual confusion in our minds. Our brains do not like this at all. Some of the emotional tolls will be manifested in the total lack of memory or remembering events wholly incorrectly. Dr. Cloud addresses this effect and calls it stagnation, seen in people whose emotional development has actually stopped at the point in which they began to escape life. They dissociate either through substances like alcohol or drugs or, in this case, through confusion, shame, and incongruent living.

Psalm 68:5-6 tells us that God will be a *Father to the fatherless, defender of widows—this is God, whose dwelling is holy. God places the lonely in families; he sets the prisoners free and gives them joy. But he makes the rebellious live in a sun-scorched land* (NLT). God will not leave us alone forever, nor will He leave us to rot in a prison of our own making if we truly wish to escape.

> *The Lord stood with me and strengthened me, so that the message might be preached fully through me, and that all the Gentiles might hear. Also I was delivered out of the mouth of the lion. And the Lord will deliver me from every evil work and preserve me for His heavenly kingdom. To Him be glory forever and ever. Amen!* (II Timothy 4:17-18, NKJV).

During the unique summer of 2020 and the worldwide pandemic shutdown, I realized that youth camps and family camp would be canceled for the year. Therefore, I wisely decided that my mother and I would make the long drive to Florida to visit my sister for the month of July. I had been quite sick with COVID-19 since March but felt somewhat good enough to make the drive.

I had been fighting a fear that overtook me in March that year when I became sick with the virus although we didn't have any tests to verify my sickness. I was still coughing and experiencing viral rebounds as my body would return to the virus again and again as if I'd been exposed to someone with the virus afresh. Since this had occurred several times since March, I was dealing with it as best I could at the time. Basically, I stayed at home, coughed my guts out, and tried to function in a somewhat (previously) normal fashion in spite of my continual symptoms most days.

We decided that we would leave for my sister's on a Monday. Lo and behold, symptoms made their appearance once again. We prayed.

We called people to pray. I walked around with my Bible held firmly to my chest and finally decided to start the trip the next morning. Before we left, I made a trip to my doctor's office to get yet another steroid shot to combat the inflammation in my airways. I crossed my fingers that nothing would worsen.

As we traveled across the state, I began feeling much worse. By the time we crossed the first state line, I had developed a fever. Remember, I had battled the worst spirit of fear I had ever known since March, and I was exhausted. I already had my seat warmer on and the air conditioner set to blow as little as possible without alerting my mother that something was very wrong.

I noticed the interstate signs for the first rest stop, so I decided to halt to take a short nap. When we stopped, I got out of the car and paced a picnic area. Earlier that morning, I had texted a few close friends with a brief explanation of my situation and asked them to pray for me. I was most terrified of my elderly mother becoming sick with the virus as she hadn't yet tested positive. Here we were, side by side in the car for at least fifteen hours for the road trip. We all know that close proximity wasn't a good situation.

As I frantically paced around the picnic table, one of my sweet friends called and another texted. The friend on the other end of the phone was righteously angry at that point. She declared what I was going to do and what God was going to do. We had a mighty prayer meeting on the phone at that rest stop that afternoon.

The other friend demanded that I create a list of words to look at while I drove. I rummaged in my backpack and found a four-by-six-inch index card. I wrote the words on the card and Exodus 15:26 on the back. After I took a quick nap, I propped that index card in front of the RPMs on my dashboard, gathered myself resolutely, and aimed the car east. I estimate that I said those words to myself at least one thousand times on that long drive to Florida. I would reach up and turn the card over to quote the Scripture on the back for a while and then flip the card again to start on the other side.

Thankfully, it rained most of the trip, so I was able to leave the AC on low. Though my symptoms did not abate, my mind remained partially sane and allowed me to find the energy my brain and body demanded to drive those hours.

Why the card? Why the verse? Why the words? I needed a mantra to get me to Florida. I desperately needed a positive soundtrack. I had to lean my mind on something that was tangible, and I already knew that the Word of God is living, powerful, and sharper than any two-edged sword. I had to keep my soul from being in control for those hours in the car, and the only thing powerful enough to beat my mind was the Word of God!

You can see the exact index card at the beginning of this chapter. It has dirt on it and I don't even care. That card will have a permanent place in my prayer book as long as I have a prayer book. I have now moved the card three times as I have created new prayer books. That card is and I hope will always be a constant fixture. It is a trophy of a time when I beat my mind at its game while utilizing my weapon of God's Word. My whole being, my soul, wanted to go crazy, but I knew I couldn't let it—at least until I got us safely to Florida!

Hopefully, that illustrates the point of this chapter. Our sound-tracks either make us or break us. For once in my life—that day on the interstate—I chose my soundtrack to make me better. I still had to drive. I was still coughing with very tight airways. But I made it with my mind intact.

Think back to the last time you made it through with your mind intact or when your mind went berserk and you lost your grip. Years ago, every time my mind went berserk, my shame increased exponentially. I might have had three good days or three months in a row, but if I allowed one thing to go wrong—Wham! Back in the swamp.

The only good news is that, over time, this whole soundtrack concept gets better and easier. Every time you will learn, and every time you will become stronger.

Renovating the Old Tunes

We have to be the boss of our mantras, the soundtracks playing in our souls. Over the years, most of us have curated some terrible soundtracks that we would be embarrassed for anyone else to hear. It's kind of like when you get your first car and discover that you can listen to any ol' ungodly thing you desire on your FM radio or Apple CarPlay because it is your car! But then, your mom impulsively (or not) opts to ride with you to church. Busted! That is how it would feel if we played some of our soundtracks as we drove our friends to church.

> If you listen to any thought long enough, it becomes a part of your personal playlist.

We must tackle the tough work of renovating our soundtracks. Acuff says to ask yourself and your soundtracks three questions:

+ Is it true?
+ Is it helpful?
+ Is it kind?

I am afraid you already know the answers if your soundtracks are anything like mine were several years ago. I could wake up and just begin thinking about my day. Almost instantly, I would begin ripping into myself about not being able to finish everything on my exhausting "must-get-done-today-at-all-costs" list. By then, my mind had picked up on the fact that stress was sending torpedoes across my body in the form of cortisol, and here we would go all over again.

Some of you might be saying, "Well, I have to talk to myself that way to get things finished!" Go back, and consider the list of three questions once again.

Perhaps right here, we should stop and add this question, "Am I giving myself grace in this moment?"

Growth Takes Time—Lots of It

I'm reasonably sure that most of us have listened to our fair share of music. Some of us might even have listened to music that wasn't edifying to our souls. Some of that music might have not been holy. I know. Most of you are just perfect and would never do such a thing as listening to—gasp!—worldly music. But, for most of us, we had to make some tough decisions eventually about the type of music we would listen to on Sirius Radio and through our AirPods. That meant we had to change some playlists. Delete some songs. Trash several based on lyrics. Hopefully, you approached these decisions with prayer and allowed the Lord to lead you instead of following what your soul impulsively told you based on the latest emotional high from that stirring altar service.

In order to renovate our foundations and drain the swamps in our lives, we have to march right in and take territory! We have to do more than just hope we will get better. Hope is never a wise strategy except in the Bible!

> *Jesus said, "The Kingdom of God is like a farmer who scatters seed on the ground. Night and day, while he's asleep or awake, the seed sprouts and grows, but he does not understand how it happens. The earth produces the crops on its own. First, a leaf blade pushes through, then the heads of wheat are formed, and finally, the grain ripens"* (Mark 4:26-28, NLT).

This is precisely what must happen with the new soundtracks in our minds. We must begin to plant tiny seeds of the Word every day. Eventually, those seeds will sprout, and we will have a new crop of stalks of wheat!

How do new crops grow? I have heard that nothing productive happens on a mountaintop. The valley is the place where things grow. We've been in the mountains in Colorado with friends. As we drove higher and higher, I realized that above the tree line, I did not see much vegetation.

Yet we constantly think that if we could just have that one huge spiritual mountaintop experience, everything would be miraculously better! We have to realize the low areas of life collect the rain. If we want growth, we have to water the plants.

Water plus dirt equals mud. Sounds like the swamp once again. If we want things to change in our lives, it must happen from a low point, and it must involve rain and mud. Stop hating yourself because of the mud! Mud is good. Mud represents new life and growth.

If we faithfully delete old soundtracks and replace those worn-out tunes with new and improved ones from the Word of God, our minds will become much better. Though simple, this concept is tough to implement because it requires tenacity and dogged determination.

Recently, I was teaching a group of ladies through Zoom and discussing this concept. After the class concluded for that month, we corresponded on a Google doc through a Q&A. One dear woman asked, "Could you explain the mantras and the Scriptures to me again, please?" Yes! For sure!

I am happy to explain again and again. To replace all the faulty and toxic mantras or soundtracks we have constantly played for years with something else takes a lot of proactive thought and effort.

For years, I have heard about the life cycle of a bamboo tree and I feel it applies well here. Replacing the old, toxic soundtracks in our souls takes time, but there is a payoff.

There's a famous analogy of life compared to a bamboo tree. The bamboo tree grows, unlike any other tree in the world. You have to water and fertilize it every day for five years and here's where it starts to get weird. Nothing happens for five years as nothing grows and it's like you are just watering the dirt. In the fifth year, the bamboo tree will break through the ground and grow eighty feet in six weeks. It's like you can see it growing right in front of your eyes. It is similar to your life, you may be doing something and not seeing anything from your effort. But deep down you know that something is happening. You are like a bamboo tree digging its roots deep into the ground. You are building the most important part of your life which is the base of the pyramid. You are learning about yourself, learning about other people, learning about what works for you or what doesn't work. So don't worry,

when the time is right everything will happen as it is supposed to.[43]

Bamboo is a symbol of longevity because of its durability,
strength, flexibility, and resilience. It survives in the harshest
conditions, still standing tall and staying green year-round.
When the storm comes, bamboo bends with the wind. When
the storm ceases, it resumes its upright position. Its ability to
cope with adversity and still stand firmly without losing its
original ground is inspirational. Its flexibility and adaptability
are a lesson to us all that the secret of a long happy life is to
go with the flow.[44]

Keep doing the hard work. Eventually, on a day when you least
expect it, you will realize you have grown. Your worn-out soundtracks are slowly moving aside for the eternally important words and
new mantras you are creating.

Defense Mechanisms

How many times did I defend myself to myself? How many times
did I act as both the judge and the defense attorney to myself in the
courtroom of my mind? While it's crazy to think about, with shame
rolling the broken, toxic soundtracks, this is an everyday occurrence.
How does our thinking get so messed up and so flawed? We know the
Scriptures, yet we do not live by the Scriptures.

This is the cognitive dissonance we have covered at length previously, but I really want you to understand this cognitive dissonance or
incongruence. The term doesn't matter. The only thing to really comprehend here is that we must begin to live what we believe. To live
what we believe, we have to believe what we say we believe. How do
we believe what we believe?

As I said before, I would teach Bible studies and tell people about
the love of God yet not feel or appropriate that love of God for myself. Oh, and God's forgiveness? No way. There is just no way God

would ever forgive me for all the rebellious actions and dumb decisions from the past, right? Okay, right here, we must focus on God's love and His forgiveness.

Wrongly, we believe we are worthless. Wrongly, we believe we are flawed and will never be capable of being vessels of honor in the house of God. This list could go on for about thirty-nine pages. Why? How did we get to this point in our relationship with God?

Let me ask you a question. How do you respond when someone gives you a sincere compliment about your hair, your outfit, or your kids actually behaving at this moment? Oh, it's okay. I think I already know this answer because I was the best at deflecting compliments to make myself seem flawed or to prove why the compliment could not possibly be true. My hair? I just popped it into a messy bun, no big deal. My outfit? Oh, yeah, I got this at Goodwill for two dollars. We assume the role of Debbie Downer to ourselves. Always and forever. Again, how do we change this behavior? Is this a defense mechanism or distorted thinking?

Matthew 7:11 speaks of receiving good things from our heavenly Father. "If you then, being evil, know how to give good gifts to your children, how much more will your Father who is in heaven give what is good to those who ask Him!" (NASB). If we know that God loves us, even as sinners, we must trust that He desires to give good things to us just because we ask.

I can hear your old soundtrack playing right now, "Yes, but, you see, I am not that good. I don't deserve anything that God gives me." Just keep reading. We will eventually get "there," you and me— wherever "there" might be.

Oversharing could also be shame behavior that is a defense mechanism. I decided to attend a multi-week training at our local not-for-profit hospice for direct patient care volunteers. This idea would prove to be unwise although I didn't see it at the time. My dad had died of cancer just two months prior, and I wasn't in the best mind-set to be learning anything new or to be working with other patients who were actively dying. However, I was sitting at the U-shaped table that Thursday night when the social worker posed a question.

I cannot remember the exact inquiry, but it fell in the category of "Why did you decide to become a volunteer for hospice?" While I listened to the others in the group, I actively pondered how I could precisely answer the question as "short and sweet" as possible. What occurred next remains a great mystery in my mind.

As I started my very precise answer, something like a geyser went off inside my mind and soul. As I talked, I started to angry cry and completely had a breakdown in front of the others in the class, as well as the directors of the hospice. I spewed the intense anger I had for my dad's oncologist and the long days we had needlessly spent in the huge hospital in Tulsa, and I expounded on my wish, formulated too late, that my dad would have been on hospice so he could die with respect at home. I was so mortified by the eruption of intense emotions that I wanted to crawl under the table and right out the front door of the facility, but I could not seem to stifle the outburst for anything that night.

I finally got myself under control and sat quietly while I wiped my face and neck from the hot tears that had been flowing. I was full of turmoil at that moment, and the question set off something explosive inside me—unresolved shame and unforgiveness. Later, the social worker kindly asked me to meet with her once a week for grief counseling, to which I agreed thankfully.

Through that experience, I learned that any pent-up shame, unforgiveness, or bitterness has the tendency to blow up at any moment in the terrible form of oversharing. Through the eruption, a person lies to herself that everything is a justified defense against what the people are saying.

While this is complicated to explain, I am sure many of you know exactly what I am attempting to express. Oversharing is never good and is most times evidence of shame.

Distorted Thinking

Recently, I was in a church service on a Sunday morning and the worship team sang a song that had such powerfully true lyrics. The piece, "Yes, He Can," by CAIN, speaks of voices that attempt to convince me I am too far from God's reach to expect help. Then, it lifts a call of victory. Our God keeps His promises, and I put my faith in Him and His Word.

Just how many times have we thought those lyrics of being too broken for God to care? We are not that much different from Adam and Eve, who hid from God. When we believe the voices in our head, shame separates us from God and makes us think that we need to hide from God, from ourselves, from other people, and from the body of Christ. Adam and Eve's biggest problem was that they lost the ability to believe God could love them after their rebellion. However, the Word of God explains His love.

> *We have come to know and have believed the love which God has for us. God is love, and the one who abides in love abides in God, and God abides in him. By this, love is perfected with us, so that we may have confidence in the day of judgment; because as He is, so also are we in this world. There is no fear in love; but perfect love casts out fear, because fear involves punishment, and the one who fears is not perfected in love. We love because He first loved us* (I John 4:16-19, NASB).

If we know that God loves us, Satan can no longer attack our belief system about the love of God. Shame has made us separated from God, which hinders our thought or sense that we feel His love. This is a very clever trick of the enemy. It is the biggest lie of all time! Chester Wright says of this lie:

It is our confidence in His love for us that is the foundation for our defense against the devil's attack of accusation and the onslaught of fear in the midst of crisis. Fear and love do not coexist. One is the absence of the other in exactly the same way that light and darkness are the opposite of the other. In fact, darkness does not exist for it is defined as the absence of light. Likewise, fear abiding in us and influencing us is the absence of love.

Even though Adam and Eve were banished from the Garden of Eden, God was still with them. He went looking for them. They felt shame. Guilt says, "I have done wrong." Shame says, "I am wrong." When God forgives us of our sins, He forgets our sins. When we have shame, we repeatedly ask God to forgive us of the same sin, day after day. God heard our prayer the first day and forgave us.

We continue to ask for forgiveness because of distorted and faulty wiring, or soundtracks that tell us God hasn't forgiven us. Micah 7:19 promises us that God will have compassion on us and that He will cast our sins into the depths of the sea.

"If there is anything in my past that I cannot think of without the memories producing feelings (pain, anger, etc.) then I am not free. I am not healed. As long as my past causes feelings, those wounds are an open door to the" voice of the devil which enables him to lie to me about me.[45] Because his lies sound and feel believable, I am ashamed. Whatever we think about the most grows, because we give it energy. "The deception of this shame paralyzes me! Shame undermines my faith, preventing God from being able to answer my prayers."[46]

Warren Wiersbe said, "When Satan wanted to lead the first man and woman into sin, he started by attacking the woman's mind." *But I am afraid that, as the serpent deceived Eve by his craftiness, your minds will be led astray from the simplicity and purity of devotion to Christ* (II Corinthians 11:3, NASB).

> Why would satan want to attack your mind? Because your mind is part of the image of God where God communicates with you and reveals His will to you. God renews our lives by renewing our minds, and He renews our minds through His truth. This truth is the Word of God.[47]

In our distorted thinking, we have to realize that shame allows Satan access to our thoughts. Your mind affects your whole being: spirit, soul, and body. Thus, when your mind is not right, nothing will be right. All of our lives, we have heard that Satan is the accuser of the brethren. (See Revelation 12:10.) The devil's goal is to sow seeds of lies to me—about myself! When we have shame, those seeds are sown in the swamp. Then, all the devil has to do is step back and watch the destructive show.

A verse of Scripture that has opened a powerful revelation to me is II Timothy 2:25-26 (NIV): *Opponents must be gently instructed, in the hope that God will grant them repentance leading them to a knowledge of the truth, and that they will come to their senses and escape from the trap of the devil, who has taken them captive to do his will.* When I oppose myself with toxic soundtracks and soul behavior from the swamp, I open a door to Satan and allow myself to be taken prisoner by his slimy self. And it gets worse, for then I run the devil's errands.

If I know anything, I know Satan is not my friend or yours. We ought not to be running errands for him! How do we disentangle ourselves from the grip of the enemy of our souls? I sincerely wish for all of us to be gently instructed by this book and other books that encourage us, but the main book for our instruction has to be the Good Book! We must desire to come to the knowledge of truth for our distorted thinking and then act on that goal, and God will allow us to come to our senses.

Perhaps it is time for you to sit with your Bible and create a list of Scriptures to push back on your distorted or faulty soundtracks. We must be able to accept God's forgiveness so that we may forgive ourselves, put the past into the past, and leave it there. At the end of this chapter, you will find an opportunity to take a few moments to let this section sink deeply into your spirit.

Neuroplasticity

Did you know that your brain and your mind are not the same? I know. Mind blown right here on aisle seven.

Dr. Caroline Leaf explains:

Your mind is not your brain, just as you are not your brain. Thoughts are located in three different places: in your brain, in the cells of your body, and in your mind. . . . The building of thoughts is called neuroplasticity. It's characterized by a triad of thinking, feeling, and choosing. When you think, you will feel, and when you think and feel, you will choose. The mind is made up of trillions and trillions of thoughts. A thought is a real physical thing that occupies mental real estate in the brain and in the mind. Thoughts look like trees. We are not prisoners to the content of our mind, whether they come in the form of an anxious thought, a depressive feeling, or a painful memory.

Neuroscientists believe that the adult brain is malleable and that it's governed by neural pathways that become deepened by our habitual thoughts. For example, when our mind defaults to the memory of feeling hurt, shame, or emptiness—to that place of not letting go—we can choose to rewire it positively. When we deepen the neural pathways in our brains, we regulate our emotions, which creates a more peaceful life.[48]

Uncontrolled, toxic thinking has the potential to create a state of low-grade inflammation across the body and the brain, affecting cortisol levels, hormones, brain functionality, and even chromosomes. . . . This toxic feedback loop between the mind and the brain and body activates the "hamster wheel" of toxic thinking, feeling and choosing.[49]

If we are what we think, just like we are what we eat, our minds must get rid of the toxins. Isaiah 26:3 says that God will *keep in perfect peace those whose minds are steadfast, because they trust in [Him]* (NIV). The Bible instructs us to have a sound mind. In order to do this, we must detox ourselves from the power that Satan has on our minds. The only way to accomplish that detox is to barrel straight through the swamp and onto the dreaded foundation renovation.

I am fairly sure we have all learned II Timothy 1:7 at some point. But do we put this into practice, and do we fully believe this passage of Scripture? Let's break down the verse.

For God has not given us a spirit of timidity, but of power and love and discipline (NASB). Go ahead and read it in your version as well—or all the versions! The Scripture declares that God has not given us a spirit of timidity, fear, or cowardice. Okay, shame, back up right there. Next, God has extended to us a spirit of power, love, and a sound mind, or a disciplined mind. A disciplined mind is a mind filled with newly created soundtracks!

When fear rules us, there is no way possible that God's love or His power can force us to have a disciplined mind. No way! At that moment, our soul is the boss, and we are living smack dab in the middle of the swamp. All the while, we peer between the cattails at everyone else and wish we were like them or that we could do the cool kingdom kid stuff they are doing.

What does it take to get to a disciplined mind? Time. Work. Constant surveillance of our thoughts until we begin to replace the broken soundtracks with new ones. The understanding of our brains, our minds, and the body connection.

My dad always taught us, "If wishes were horses, beggars would ride." We can try to wish shame away, but it is quite insidious. It will just stay until we rewire and completely reshape our thoughts. "Life isn't about wishing you were somewhere or someone you're not. Life is about enjoying where you are, loving who you are, and consistently improving both."[50]

One of the reasons I feel so passionate about this section of the book is because of my long and arduous journey with my own toxic thoughts. If I had known or someone had taught me this in the first thirty-five years of life, I would have been able to save so much valuable time. I could have spared so many people the fallout from my toxic, faulty soundtrack self.

Who Am I in Christ?

I am a light in the world—Matthew 5:14
I am a child of God—John 1:12
I am Christ's friend—John 15:15

101

I am chosen and appointed by Christ to bear fruit—John 15:16
I am a member of Christ's body—I Corinthians 12:27;
Ephesians 5:30
I am a member of reconciliation—II Corinthians 5:18-19
I am righteous and holy—Ephesians 4:24
I am chosen and dearly loved—Colossians 3:12
I am a saint—Ephesians 1:18; II Corinthians 1:1-2
I am born of God and the evil one cannot touch me—I John 5:18
I am forgiven and freely forgive others—Matthew 6:14-15
I am victorious—I John 5:4
I am prospered by God—He cares for me!—III John 2
I have died to myself so Christ is fully alive through me—
Galatians 2:20
I have been given enough manna for today—Exodus 16:21
I am born again—I Peter 1:23

Reflection

1. Name some of the toxic soundtracks that your mind has played on repeat for a while.
2. What are you thinking about the growth, healing, and restoration that must take place in you? Are you ready or resistant?
3. What are some of your distorted thoughts about the Word of God? What have you distorted in your mind about God and His Word?
4. Do you believe that your brain can rewire your thought patterns with new soundtracks?
5. Do you really believe that you could be whole again—your inner man renewed with a robe of righteousness?

Atonement

My Grandma Harger was a fierce and independent woman who believed God's Word could heal by application of the Scripture. Whenever anyone would get cut and begin bleeding for any reason, she would go to her Bible and find Leviticus 17:11. She would read, "For the life of the flesh is in the blood, and I have given it to you upon the altar to make atonement for your souls; for it is the blood that makes atonement for the soul" (NKJV).

As a young child, I wrote this verse and the phrase, "The life is in the blood," in the opening pages of my Bible. My grandma believed something powerful. She had been taught by someone that the Word of God was powerful enough to stop bleeding.

As a kid, I usually kind of smirked and thought all the drama was quite silly, but she was a believer in the concept and the Scripture. Right now, I cannot remember if the blood was ever actually stopped by her reading this verse or not. That is not really the point.

The point is that the Word of God works and has atoning power to heal all manner of life's hurts, bleeding wounds, and cuts of the heart and soul. You know, those death-by-a-thousand-cuts type of situations. Yeah, the Word of God works on those also.

Faith in the Word of God

As I stated earlier, for so long I was a good parrot. In other words, I could recite the Word of God, but I did not apply it to my own heart. Nor did I truly believe in its powerful work in my own life.

At Easter, we all celebrate the symbolic cross and the resurrection of Jesus Christ. As a member of ministry, I can say that sometimes Easter would come and go. Only later did I realize that I had never taken the time to consider the significance of what Jesus Christ did for me and how my life has the potential to be completely different, all because of the cross and the empty tomb. My question is this—do we truly believe in the power of that cross and the empty tomb? I would say, not so much.

It is my humble opinion that our view of God is mostly distorted, depending on our backgrounds, our mind-sets, our level of shame, and our belief systems. So much hangs on our view of God and His power to save us, heal us, and deliver us. Obviously, this entire book would be completely unnecessary if we all possessed a healthy view of God and His Word and a healthy, scriptural view of ourselves.

Brené Brown claims the antidote for shame is empathy. I understand her viewpoint. She is the premier researcher of shame and needs an antidote to offer everyone who reads her books and watches her TED talks. However, I disagree. I must disagree because the Word teaches something entirely different.

I feel the church at large has gotten itself into some murky swamp waters when dealing with all things pertaining to soul behavior. These include mind matters, heart matters, and behaviors. We are freely using terms like anxiety, panic attacks, depression, church hurt, and many others. I understand. You might have all of these words. I am by no means making light of or trying to discount your hurt or your anxiousness at all. Please hear me out. Allow me to explain myself in this chapter before you toss these words into a trash can.

During my twenty-plus years of experience teaching elementary school, I understood something about kiddos and the learning-to-read process. For example, if I was teaching second grade and had a student consistently underperforming on phonics and reading fluency assessments, I would suggest some things to the student's family that might have seemed a bit in left field.

I would ask the family if the student had been to the ophthalmologist for an eye exam and if it was possible that the student was experiencing difficulty seeing words or letters on a page. I would ask the family if the student had been to visit the pediatrician to have his or her ears checked for hearing difficulties. I would inquire what kind of breakfast food the student was eating and or how much sleep he or she usually got on a school night. Over the years, I was astounded at how many times these simple questions completely fixed the student's reading problem.

The same is true here. How many times do we run too quickly to a solution that is outside the Word of God? How many times do we run to Google or Pinterest? I love both of those tools, but there are times only faith in the Word of God will fix the issue. As far as counseling, I am all for folks receiving godly wisdom to help them solve hurts and hang-ups.

Again, my issue is not with counseling. My issue is with running to fix something that is broken in our lives without learning to lean on the Word of God while putting some faith in action and allowing God the opportunity to fix some of these things. That is exactly what we're going to put to use here. We are going to the Word of God.

My Healing

For years, I was sick. Really sick. The intense coughing began one winter season with bronchitis and seemed to have a recurrence every winter season. Every time I would have longer bouts of coughing. When I say, "coughing," I mean the kind of fits that would break blood vessels in my eyes and face and cause all sorts of plumbing leaks. This went on for many years, and the cough just continued to worsen every year.

Finally, in the spring of 2009, I was diagnosed with cryptococcal pneumonia. This simply meant that I had black mold in my lungs. It appeared out of nowhere on a chest X-ray that spring and looked like someone had sprinkled black pepper on my lungs. I mean, a lot of black pepper.

Through a really long series of doctors, hospitals, trips back and forth to the research hospital in my state, and countless diagnostic tests like bronchoscopies and CT scans, I landed at the National Jewish Health Respiratory Hospital in Denver, Colorado, in the spring of 2012. The hospital in Denver is the best respiratory hospital in the USA, and I would highly recommend that facility to anyone needing diagnoses. There, I was diagnosed with severe reactionary cough-variant asthma and vocal cord dysfunction.

Regardless of all they did to help, I still coughed. I finally had some procedures and surgeries to correct minor ailments that had happened from the severe coughing. Still, I was sick, and the coughing had not ceased.

For the next few years, I would struggle with vocal cord problems and voice issues. I endured weeks of total voice rest, which translated into zero talking. Occurrences like grass-fire smoke in the air brought on bouts of high heart rate and emergency room visits. Anything in the air could irritate my airways, even powdered lemonade mix or fajita smoke in a Mexican restaurant.

At this point, I had learned much about myself through the sickness and had discovered a love for the Word of God that I never had before. Some days I could do nothing physically except sit with my Bible and read. I missed more days of school on sick leave than I had missed in my entire teaching career. I had always wished to be able to read my Bible through but found myself stymied. During the years of physical weakness, my wish was granted as I was able to read my Bible through multiple times each year.

Please don't feel sorry for me. That sickness and the respiratory hospital in Denver saved me. God's mercy supplied His process that I had to journey through to get to the other side of the swamp. Those years were the healing process that led me out of the swamp and through my own version of the wilderness.

Without those difficult years of chronic sickness and total dependence on God, I would not be the person I am today. I am thankful for the cough and for the many, many desolate days alone at my house. I learned numerous invaluable lessons from the Lord and His Word in that time of isolation and aloneness with God that simply could not have been learned any other way.

Fast forward to an Oklahoma Ministers' Retreat in 2014. A missionary was the Saturday morning devotion speaker. He wasn't even supposed to be there if I remember correctly, but he was filling in for a preacher who was unexpectedly unable to attend. Nathan Harrod preached a simple message about healing and the power of God to heal and deliver.

I heard it but only halfheartedly. I had been prayed for so many times over the previous years that I was almost without hope. While the National Jewish Hospital in Denver had worked to improve my health, I was still sick and having trouble living day-to-day life. At the end of Missionary Harrod's message, he said something shocking that I haven't forgotten. He instructed, "Don't come to the front to be prayed for. Come to the front to be healed."

Right then, I had to make a choice. I desperately wanted to stay at my seat, be the victim, and insist, "Well, I've been prayed for a lot, and nothing has worked yet." Remember, I was working through a lot of distorted thinking about God and His Word, so this was a huge test of faith for me.

I quickly decided to step to the front to be healed. As I neared the front, Missionary Harrod gave directions. He was not dramatic or sensational about anything. As I look back, I realize this was beneficial to me.

A lady I knew only slightly came to stand in front of me to pray the prayer of faith for me. As she prayed for me, I began feeling a strange sensation in my chest cavity from my throat area down to my waistline. I felt as if a grass fire burned very hotly inside my chest cavity. I even stopped the lady and said, "I think there's something wrong here, and we might have to stop praying."

At that moment, Missionary Harrod said, "Sometimes when God heals someone, he or she might feel a strong burning sensation and feel uncomfortable, but don't stop praying!" So the lady kept praying.

That day, I walked away believing in healing, but due to my past and all the mind struggles, I was almost hesitant to receive fully and believe in my miracle. A few weeks later, I realized I had not experienced a single episode of coughing, suffered from any coughing fits, or had any emergency room visits. I had been completely healed that Saturday morning.

Missionary Harrod was not the one who healed me. Rather, the saving power of the blood of Jesus Christ accomplished the miracle. Jesus had completely healed me! Even as I type this, I am overcome with thankfulness and emotion about how magnificent God has shown Himself in and to me!

Revelation of the Cross

On April 27, 2018, I heard a message preached by Dr. James Hughes that would forever alter the way I thought of the Cross, "The Power of the Cross." I wish I could point you to a video, but all I have are my notes and an mp4 I purchased at the event. These next several points are from my notes gleaned during his powerful message that was so revelatory to me.

The Cross is not a revelation of your horrible past and your past sins. The reason our lives are full of chaos is that we are living out the prophecy we believe or think about ourselves. This becomes a self-fulfilling prophecy.

Dr. Hughes said that the Catholic church convinced us that the Cross makes us worthless. The Cross is not about my worthlessness. It's not an exposé of my past or my badness. Instead, the Cross is all about value and God's desire for each of us to have a revelation of where He wants to take us.

> *Therefore we also, since we are surrounded by so great a cloud of witnesses, let us lay aside every weight, and the sin which so easily ensnares us, and let us run with endurance the race that is set before us, looking unto Jesus, the author and finisher of our faith, who for the joy that was set before Him endured the cross, despising the shame . . .* (Hebrews 12:1-2, NKJV).

Paul, the lawyer, began with a position that the cross was the joy set before Jesus Christ. Why did Christ have joy at the cross before

Him? Remember Genesis? Because of the sin committed, mankind lost its rightful ownership of authority, identity, and dominion. Jesus endured the cross so that we might be reconciled back to Him and His atoning power, which would return us to the original authority, identity, and dominion. We are looking unto Jesus, the author and finisher of our faith.

After we have been baptized in His name, our sins are covered with the blood Jesus Christ shed on Calvary. We enter a solemn and binding covenant with Jesus Christ only through His shed blood. That covenant is a binding contract

> It doesn't matter how big God is; how I view myself in God is how I will live in Him.

that tells us we now live in a community together as one body of believers in Christ. Yesterday is covered with His blood, so neither I nor you are able to see the sin anymore. The only thing I am able to see is how valuable I am to the kingdom.

To be fully healed of shame, we must all come to this truth. We must begin to comprehend our value and our worth to the King of kings and to ourselves. No more living in incongruence; rather, living with fully open arms that embrace the validity of the Word of God.

What Is Atonement?

In the Old Testament, a large structure covered by several animal skins was called the Tabernacle. While the Israelites wandered in the wilderness for forty years, God directed Moses to manufacture this structure. There, God's Presence would be manifest after the blood of the bulls and goats was correctly applied to the different pieces of furniture. One piece of furniture was the brazen altar, where animals were sacrificed for the sins of the people.

In the inner room of that Tabernacle, a veil separated a holy place from the Holy of Holies. God demonstrated His power and glory in that most holy place. The piece of furniture adorning that sanctuary was the ark of the covenant. Along the sides of the golden rectangle, cherubim physically covered the middle, the mercy seat (Hebrews 9:5). The mercy seat served as the lid of the ark of the covenant.

That top was the place of atonement. Once a year, the high priest was commanded to sprinkle blood from the spotless lamb onto the mercy seat. This action made atonement for the sins of the people but only once a year. Annually, their sins were pushed ahead for another year but never permanently removed.

Romans 3:25 tells us that Jesus was the propitiation, or grace, we receive through faith in his blood. This means Jesus became the Lamb of God and stood in the place of the countless animals sacrificed in the years of the past. When Jesus Christ was the Lamb, our sins were remitted and gone forever!

When our sins are atoned by the blood of Jesus through baptism in His name, we are invited to participate in the holy covenant of the blood shed for our sins. For sins to be remitted, blood must be shed. We learned that in the Book of Genesis. The same applies today.

This concept of a Savior dying on the cross for my sins and then rising from the dead so that I might have everlasting life is almost incomprehensible. The amazing part is that my life has been atoned, and I am now free from every curse, sin, and every bit of the power of the enemy of my soul. The blood goes before and beyond my sins.

We have been redeemed by the precious blood of the unblemished and spotless Lamb (I Peter 1:18-19). The same blood that was applied to the mercy seat buys my freedom each day from sin, fear, rejection, perfection, lying, incongruence, and approval. The list is long, but the covenantal blood will outlast any sin. Many are free from the jail of sin but are still imprisoned by soulish behavior, which has already been atoned by the blood of Jesus Christ.

A few months ago at a coffee shop, I saw a T-shirt with this message: "Don't trip on what's behind you!" At first, I snickered and thought, *How does someone trip on something behind him?* I could probably make that happen as klutzy as I am at times.

Then, I soberly realized that many who attend church faithfully on Sundays and Wednesdays do this very thing. I have a bad feeling that some people have been set free by the blood of Jesus Christ, but they're still imprisoned by their own doing and thinking. They are tripping on everything that is behind them. As if they sit at the gate of the prison, they can't move forward into their kingdom purpose. Our sins have been atoned by the sacrifice of the blood of Jesus Christ, the spotless Lamb of God, and have been permanently forgotten as far as the east is from the west (Psalm 103:12).

However, like myself, many have somehow missed the revelation of the power of the blood and the fact that "life is in the blood." Faith must be involved in this process, and that might happen through what we speak and how we speak over ourselves and our families. Instead of continuing to trip over everything—tiny or huge—behind us that is also behind the Cross of Jesus Christ, we must realize that the moment we asked Jesus to forgive us of our sins, He actually did.

When we are mired in the swamp of shame, we repeatedly ask God to forgive us of sins that were committed years ago. There were days when I asked Jesus to forgive me of the same sins hundreds of times. Each time, I sank a bit deeper into the muck of the swamp as I felt that Jesus wasn't forgiving me. Why? Shame constantly tells us that we are bad and wrong; therefore, God won't forgive us of sins.

My plea for forgiveness was stuck on repeat in the faulty soundtrack in my mind. God heard me the first time I asked, yet I continued to beg as if I had never asked for forgiveness of my sins. Those sins were not even a blip on God's radar because He is so powerful that He chose to forget every one of them. I had heard about the Cross all my life, but until I received a revelation of the atoning power of the blood of Jesus, the price He paid for my sin, I was stuck in the loop.

Let's consider Peter, one of the first disciples chosen by Jesus. He was mired in shame after he denied Christ. Of course, when Jesus told him that he would deny Him, Peter, just like us, argued with the Lord and said, "Lord, I will never deny You!" By Mark 14:72, we find Peter weeping bitterly as the cold, hard truth stared him in the face: he had denied the Lord.

After Jesus Christ's death and resurrection, we see Peter running ahead of the others as they set marathon records to get to the tomb to see if those crazy ladies were delusional or actually telling the truth (Luke 24:12). Then, in John 21:15-17, we have a tender moment between Peter and Jesus when Jesus tried to talk sense into Peter's hard head about his shame. Jesus asked, "Simon, do you love Me?"

"Of course, Lord!" Even as Simon Peter said the words, he struggled to comprehend how Jesus could love him after his very public failure and denial. In John 21:22, Jesus once again told Peter to follow Him and not worry about the other disciples. Jesus was working hard to make sure that Peter understood His forgiveness and atoning power that forgave the disciple his denial and colossal failure.

To make sure you get this important point, Jesus has already done that very thing for all of us. His Word has given us many promises to make sure we comprehend the atoning power of His blood and forgiveness of sins.

A while back, I was privileged to attend a conference and heard the most amazing testimony. I asked the gal to send me her written testimony. I have decided to include her story here even though she didn't have a clue what I was writing. God is cool like that. I think it is important that you hear another story besides the one I am telling throughout this book. Her story is heart-wrenching but filled with God's grace.

I was born and raised in an Apostolic church. I knew right from wrong, yet I struggled with things. In my younger years, I really loved living for God. I received the Holy Ghost when I was thirteen years old. I was so excited to be baptized shortly afterward. I wanted to be just like my pastor's wife! One day I would grow up, go to Bible college, marry a preacher, have kids, write amazing books, and speak at ladies' conferences all over the world. Then came high school.

High school was a struggle. I made friends easily enough, but I stuck out like a sore thumb as the only Pentecostal girl. I felt like an outsider. I didn't have a love for holiness or anything modest, and it showed. My parents tried, but I still wore clothes as tight as they could possibly be.

At eighteen, I met someone in the church and was allowed to go on my first date. I tried to live for God but felt myself slipping further away. My parents could see that I was not in a good place spiritually, so they took me to a conference where I would be in for a rude awakening.

There was this boy I'd had a crush on for years. He attended the same church as my family in that state. His mom came to me one evening and said she'd like to talk to me. I was slightly terrified but sat with her anyway.

She looked me in the eye and told me point-blank that she would never allow her son to date me. Her son deserved a girl who dressed godly. She had tears pouring down her face as she talked about her love for God and for modesty. I was shaken. Was I a disappointment to God? This conversation lit a spark in me. I began to pray and ask God to help me see modesty as seriously as that woman did. I felt refreshed and on fire for God.

I would like to say that I lived perfectly from that point forward, but unfortunately, that's not the case. About a year later, I was once again struggling. I was discouraged, weak, and making horrible decisions. I continued to go to church and even helped sing at church while living a life of sin. Sin is sin. I knew what I was doing and God knew. I lied to family and friends. I pretended like everything was fine, but sin compounds sin. It grew and grew. I was too ashamed to tell the truth and too caught up in the sin to get out. Something had to give or I knew I wouldn't make it with God this way.

That relief soon came in the form of a breakup. Once again, I had chosen the wrong guy. He was in church, looked the part, and had everything going for him, and I thought we would probably get married. I had gotten so caught up in this relationship that it began to take precedence over every other aspect of my life—over my family, friends, and even church.

Even while living in sin, I could feel God tugging at me. He never stopped. I was absolutely miserable and tired of being torn in two directions all the time.

The boyfriend finally threatened to break up because I refused to cut ties with my dad, whom my boyfriend hated. When the break happened, the relief was immediate. I knew it was the right thing to do. That break became permanent.

I was ready to live for God and be done with the guilt and shame that plagued the life I had been living. I repented and felt amazing. I truly knew the mercy of God and was able to trust that my sins were under the blood. I was on cloud nine for about two weeks before feeling slightly panicked that I was going to end up an old maid.

You can imagine how ecstatic I was to receive a phone call from the other guy, the one on whom I'd always had that crush. During prayer, God had given him three different signs that we were meant to be together. What? Life was finally coming together, and I just knew he was the "one." We talked on the phone for a few weeks. Then, his mom called to ask if I could help at an event in their state. I was so excited.

This was mid-year, and things were happening fast! His mom wanted us to be married before the end of the year! My parents, a bit less excited than myself, drove me to the event. Once again, we stayed with family. The next morning, I awakened to my phone blowing up. It was my ex-boyfriend.

Things got messy quickly. Of course, he was angry that I had moved on and threatened to drive to our location to tell everyone all of the things I had hidden to this point. I was too ashamed to tell my parents because I didn't want to face the disappointment I knew they would feel.

I was sobbing uncontrollably when my dad walked in. My dad was concerned and wrapped his arms around me in a huge hug. My dad held me tightly as I poured out my sins. My voice broke as I told him. Instead of letting me go in disgust, his arms tightened as if he held on for dear life.

My mom came in and about fainted, and Dad told her to give me a minute. Then, I took my mom to the guest room and told her what was happening. She laid on the bed and wept. Though their disappointment was tangible, their love was stronger, and I felt it more.

We discussed what to do as a family and decided it best to ignore the ex for now and just take the opportunity to talk to the new guy as soon as possible. We got dressed and went to the event. I sang on the praise team, but you can imagine the extreme stress I felt knowing what was coming afterward. God had given him three signs, his parents approved, and I was confident everything would be okay in the end.

I took the first opportunity to speak to him on the way to dinner as his sister and her husband chauffeured us. It was our first official date, and I should have been excited but was sick to my stomach. I was whispering my list of sins as they drove us along. I am sure they thought we were whispering sweet nothings, but it was anything but that. He told me everything was okay, and we moved on. I felt such relief. Everyone who needed to know about my sins had the information.

We got through dinner, and when we met again with my parents, he asked my dad for permission to marry me. My dad loved him and gave his consent.

On our drive back home, my ex-boyfriend continued to call, threaten me, and cause unnecessary drama. On the way home, my "future husband" called to say that since things were so crazy, we should take five days to pray and fast. I happily agreed.

Five days seems like a lifetime when you are praying and fasting for an answer from God. I felt amazing and knew the phone call would be good news. The call came—two days late. The moment of truth. He took a deep breath and then shattered my world in just a few words.

Actually, he asserted, it was in fact not God's will that we be married. He felt a call to ministry, and I was not good for ministry. "I am sorry. Keep your head up, and have a great life. Good-bye."

I didn't have to say a word. My parents knew by the tears in my voice what had happened. Shame overwhelmed me. How could I have been so naive to think that God still loved me and wanted to use me for His kingdom in any way? I was dirty, and there wasn't enough perfect blood to change that.

I fell deeply into that shame and self-pity, and I didn't see a way out. I gave up. I clearly didn't recognize the voice of God at all because it had been telling me something very different from what God had told the guy. I couldn't be forgiven of my sin. How foolish of me to ever think such a thing! A terrible downward spiral that ensued brought only additional shame and guilt.

My parents and my pastor, to whom I had come clean, loved me hard through every step. They never gave up on me although I had given up on myself. My pastor kept me on the praise team, but I felt guilty and out of place up there. That was a ministry, and I was no good for it. Someone at work asked me about church, but I felt like a hypocrite to invite the person. Witnessing was a ministry, and I was no good for it. Shame and guilt were all I felt and, quite frankly, what I deserved to feel—so I thought.

December came. If I hadn't made such horrible decisions in the past, I would have been getting married this month. Worthless. Worthless. Worthless. My mom was extremely worried about me at this point and asked me to go to a holiday youth convention with her. I agreed to appease her but really didn't see the point.

The preacher went on and on about the love of God. To be honest, I was feeling frustrated because he just kept repeating, "God still loves you! You haven't gone too far. Your sin is not too great!"

Would whomever this guy is talking to please get hold of it so this poor man can move on? I thought. I mean, his veins were popping out of his neck, for crying out loud! Now, God had never spoken to me, but I felt a chill run over my body as if the breath of God brushed my skin and whispered, "He's talking to you."

I stood and began to sob. My mom held me and prayed over me. I felt the touch of God but felt too ashamed to allow myself really to pray like I wanted. I just wept and felt I did not have the right to ask for forgiveness.

I decided that God loved me, and that was fine. I also decided that I wanted to live for Him whether I could truly be saved or not. Even though I felt shame over my past, I wanted a future that was free from it. I attended church. I loved God. I tried to be modest. I was content. I even prayed and told God how great He was. I told Him how much His mercy meant to me, but I was too ashamed actually to ask for it to cover my past.

What's funny (ironic) now is that He had already covered my past, months before—before I was told I was no good for ministry. He had already washed that sin away. My own shame brought it back up.

It took me a while, but one day, I found myself face down on the carpet in my bedroom, broken and weeping and speaking in a heavenly language. I realized that God never gave up on me. He kept tugging at my heart and gently loving me until I finally allowed myself to step into His mercy.

No sin is too great that His mercy can't cover. Shame will try to tell you otherwise, but don't listen to it. Just trust the whisper that He loves you.

I met my husband the following year. I didn't want to. It just happened. There was no chaos. He wasn't trying to tell me what God's will was for my life. After we had talked for a few months, I decided that he should know what he was getting. Yes, I was forgiven, but I felt that whomever I married deserved to know the truth. I was scared I would receive the same response as before because I knew this man also had a call to ministry. But I was determined to let him make the choice no matter what that meant for me.

He sat in silence long enough to make me uncomfortable before asking if I had repented, if I felt I'd been forgiven, and if I had truly prayed through to the Holy Ghost. To all of these, I shakily replied, "Yes."

His response was one that still blows my mind. He said, "If you're good enough for God, then you are good enough for me."

I married that man two years later. He has never brought up my past or even asked me questions about it. Just like God, he forgave me and let it go. My past doesn't define my worth in the kingdom or the ministry where God has placed me. The Word of God does not lie when it offers the promise in Proverbs 28:13, "No one who conceals transgressions will prosper, but one who confesses and forsakes them will obtain mercy" (my paraphrase).

Shame tried to stop me from being open about my past, but once I came clean about it to the right people, they held me accountable and encouraged me to keep living for God. If you tell someone your sins and he or she makes you feel like you are no good, please do not accept that as your final answer. That shameful thinking is a lie from the devil. Surround yourself with safe people. Dig into God's Word to find that His mercy endures forever.

This gal has not read this chapter or this book, but God already knew. When I heard the testimony, God spoke to me, "Include that." Take this as your confirmation that God loves you and He has already forgiven you of your sins. All the sins.

How Do We Get There?

"There" is a place of full confidence I am not sure we ever find. We sure enough cannot find it with the help of a GPS. It seems that

I search for it and end up traveling sideways and backward before finally getting totally lost from the pathway. But we will eventually get to a place where we can rest in the Lord and know with all assurance that we have been touched and healed by the power of the Cross. When we live in a community through the covenant of the blood of Jesus Christ that cannot be lightly broken, we have an obligation to the body of believers to love, to be free of any hurtful behavior, and to celebrate together as they did in the Bible!

How do we apply the power of atonement to our spirits, souls, and bodies? I firmly believe that shame is only resolved when we receive a revelation of the miracle-working power of the blood of Jesus Christ and His atoning power for us. I also believe this takes time. It is a process that all of us must submit to even though we would rather just have miraculous healing and be delivered of shame instantly.

Again, this process will take time and a lot of work. Of course, God is able to do anything as I mentioned above. But it takes all of us a long time to abandon the distorted view of ourselves so God will be merciful and allow us to unwind and remove the grave clothes ourselves, just like Lazarus needed loosening in John 11.

When Jesus finally showed up at the tomb of their brother, Mary and Martha were quite miffed with Jesus that He had not shown up earlier, so much so that they made Jesus cry. Okay, I realize Jesus was actually crying about their unbelief at that moment. After some discussion with the sisters, Jesus commanded Lazarus to come forth from the grave. That must have been quite an earth-shaking moment when the stone was rolled away and Lazarus stumbled into the blinding sunlight.

When he appeared, he wore the very grave clothes in which the sisters had tearfully dressed him just four days earlier. In verse 44, Jesus commanded, "Loose him, and let him go!"

Lazarus could have said, "No, thanks, I like these grave clothes. Please don't help me get free of these stinky strips of cloth."

Just like Lazarus, many of you are being called out of your tomb, and your grave clothes are still wrapped tightly around you. How will you choose to get free of the grave clothes? Will you work to loose your bands yourself, or will you allow yourself to be vulnerable in a community of trusted friends? Will you begin the healing process by speaking the blood of Jesus over your life—over all the wounds, uneven places, hurts, hang-ups, and unhealthy thought patterns?

The interesting thing that happened when Lazarus was brought forth from the tomb was that many people believed in Jesus afterward. When they witnessed the mighty miracle of his resurrection, they were able to believe for themselves. How many people in your sphere of influence would be healed if you would step forward into the light of Christ and claim your healing?

So the question. What will it take for you to believe in Jesus and His atoning power? He is commanding you to come forth and to live fully once again. But you have to remove your own grave clothes and be willing to live in the power of your resurrection, knowing that you have been covered by the blood of the Lamb.

Broken? No, Thanks!

We all want joy. I am sure that you just laughed and thought, *Nah, not me! That's too ridiculous even to wish for at this point.* But we sure don't want to be broken anymore.

Brokenness just sounds terrible. That sounds like we have been run over by a team of wild horses and left for dead. We want to be better, not broken! Why broken? Why don't we ever talk about being broken as a positive thing?

"Brokenness molds our character closer to the character of God than anything else. To experience defeat, disappointment, loss—the raw ingredients of brokenness—moves us closer to being like God than the victory, gain, and fulfillment ever can."

Brokenness has nothing to do with material property. It does not come from having much or no money. Some folks assume wealthy people aren't broken due to their money. But brokenness does not come from sadness or a wretched life. And vice versa. Wrong.

Brokenness is living completely submitted to God and having a contrite spirit, realizing that God has full control and access to my life.

His strength is made perfect in our weakness. Weakness is not bad. For too long, we have relied on our own strength and what we could accomplish through our soul strength. Brokenness is allowing what is inside me to be broken open so that everything inside can fully live in God's presence.

Psalm 34:18 says that to be contrite is to remorseful and repentant and to show a desire for atonement. Isaiah 57:15 calls us to possess a contrite and humble spirit. According to II Corinthians 12:9-10, brokenness is made perfect and possible only through His strength. Romans 12:1 commands us to present ourselves as living sacrifices to the Lord.

Many times, God is unable to pry open our potential in His kingdom fully because we refuse to be broken and contrite. We are opting to live in our mess, our swamp of shame. We think God doesn't like us or that He refuses to allow us to be used in His kingdom because we're flawed. But it could be that we refuse to live broken before Him. Complete surrender to Jesus Christ and His atoning blood and a commitment to live in the covenantal blessings of His death on the cross allow us complete access to everything in God's kingdom.

We all have two parts: An inner man and an outer man. Another way to say this would be soul and spirit. Romans 7:22 and Ephesians 3:16 speak of the inward man. The Holy Ghost dwells in our spirit, the inward man. Our emotions, will, and thoughts reside in the soul part as we discussed in an earlier chapter. As we have noted previously, incongruence happens when we allow the constant struggle between the guy inside who wants to serve God and the guy outside who doesn't think he's perfect enough or ever will be perfect enough for God and His Kingdom.

The toughest part of brokenness is admitting to God that you need a savior. Shame tells us that we must take care of everything on our own and not allow anyone to help us as we must be doing all the serving and helping everyone else. Shame tells us that we are strong on our own and independent. Shame tells us that we are too far gone for God to help us now, so don't try. Shame tells us, like Peter, that everyone saw your failure, so it's too late.

When we finally allow ourselves to become broken in His presence, we open our spirits to God and permit Him to help us, heal us, and deliver us like only He can.

The entire premise of brokenness rests on this passage: *Most assuredly, I say to you, unless a grain of wheat falls into the ground and dies, it remains alone; but if it dies, it produces much grain. He who loves his life will lose it, and he who hates his life in this world will keep it for eternal life* (John 12:24-25, NKJV). Jesus referred to nature, of course. In order for seeds to become plants, the shell of the seed must break to allow the water to begin the growing process.

Some examples in nature include:

+ Some seeds break open only when the water on the inside of the seed freezes and then expands, which breaks the shell.
+ Some seeds use the abuse of being pulled down a rocky river to have the wall of the shell compromised enough to allow water in.
+ Some have an outer shell that animals find tasty, and they eat the outer shell but leave the actual seed.
+ The most common example is an animal that will eat the seed, and through the digestive process, it will break down the wall of the shell.

The truth is, if we aren't broken, the inner man will never grow. We must break through that tough outer shell of shame, and that is often quite a job. Commonly, the breaking process in nature is a violent one but produces beauty, food, and productivity when it is completed. The seed wall is not precious, but it serves a purpose.

There were many different types of vessels in the Bible. The vessels weren't precious; the contents were, like the alabaster box in the Gospels. On that occasion, Jesus was approaching death on the cross. The process of brokenness says, "Not my will, but Thine be done." The cross is a reminder that Jesus had to allow the breaking of the outer man, so we must all take up our crosses and allow ourselves to be broken.[51]

God allows people to help Him break us from the control of the outer man or the soul-in-control-man. I am sure that all of us have been crucified by people who have wounded us. Jesus allows people in leadership—and sometimes even sinners—to bring change to us. But we chafe and complain our way right out of the change, so upset about the treatment from the people that we entirely miss out on what God is attempting to accomplish in our lives.

Biblical Examples of Brokenness

Samuel rebuked Saul in I Samuel 15:19-21 for his disobedience. Nevertheless, Saul, living according to the behavior of his soul and in constant rebellion against the man of God, refused to be broken.

David was confronted by the prophet in II Samuel 12:9-13. After Nathan's scathing message, David repented and was broken. We can read his prayer of brokenness or his plea for forgiveness in Psalm 51. Like David, we must change our attitude when we feel like someone is attacking us. Our attitude shouldn't be one of retaliation but rather one of humility and asking God, "What are You trying to teach me through this pain?" This is the antidote to pride and shame.

We must begin to allow every situation to strip the seed covering that is the outer man. Brokenness changes our situations. God had to break Jacob's natural strength so He could clothe him with power. Moses struck the rock with his rod, and cool water flowed from the broken stone. When Gideon and his little army broke their pitchers, the hidden light was visible. The poor widow broke the seal on the pot of oil and poured it out so God was able to use it to pay all her bills. Jesus broke the five loaves, and once they were broken, they fed five thousand men. Only when Mary broke the alabaster box did the perfume fill the room. Jesus allowed His body to be broken at the cross, and salvation flowed from His precious body.

Do you see the pattern? We must die to ourselves before we are useful to Him. We must die to all of our flaws, faults, hang-ups, distortions, approval addictions, perfectionism, control, and on and on. Without brokenness there is no authority, there is no provision, there is no witness, there are no blessings, there is no true worship, and there is no salvation.

God uses the broken. He wants you usable for Him. Brokenness is the place where God can be God alone—not in competition with you for control or for perfection in your life. He should not have to compete with you as you seek approval from all the people.

> Do not be afraid of the Saturday in your faith. Within a story where the cross could have led to a resurrection on the same exact day, God planted a Saturday. A day of mourning. Of confusion. Suspension and weeping. Of questioning. Of loss. Things die and we must mourn what could have been and what we thought was supposed to be. It takes time for new things to grow from fallow ground. What grows in the low points of our faith is not the same stuff that grows in the high points. It's okay to hold both grief and mustard seeds in the same hand.[52]

Joy Is Possible after the Resurrection

You can and will find peace and joy in the kingdom. Hebrews 12:2 cites the example of Jesus to teach us that joy comes after we have been willing to lay down our lives for Jesus Christ. Psalm 51:12-13 offers the prayer, *Restore to me the joy of Your salvation And sustain me with a willing spirit. Then I will teach transgressors Your ways, And sinners will be converted to You* (NASB).

What is genuine joy in the Lord? Joy equals gratitude. Joy equals strength. Remember that the kingdom of God is counterculture to this world's way of thinking and doing things. The antidote for sadness is not joy. Joy happens when we follow God's plan of atonement and brokenness in our lives.

I love to compare Psalm 51 and Joel 2 because they both demonstrate that after the removal of shame and the restoration of joy, we will be thrilled to move into our God-given purpose of teaching His ways to those not yet like Him. The amazing understanding or revelation that Jesus Christ died for my sins and did that while I was yet in my sin defines love as it was meant to be. Purpose follows brokenness, and joy follows restoration. Joy destroys access to depression, frustration, and exhaustion. Peace and joy are often paired in our hearts. When I experience peace, I usually have joy, and vice versa.

At this point, I trust and wildly hope that you are well on your way to finding a slightly lit pathway through the dark, scary swamp. The trail will eventually lead you to your divine kingdom purpose.

Baby Steps to Wholeness

The first step is to rediscover who God is to you, His ways, and His kingdom. Take a moment to read these verses:

✦ I Corinthians 4:20
✦ I Corinthians 2:4-5
✦ Zechariah 4:6
✦ Matthew 12:28
✦ Luke 11:20
✦ Luke 9:1-2
✦ Luke 10:8-9

Along the margin here, write your thoughts about the kingdom of God from the above list of verses.

The second step is believing that we are made righteous only by Jesus Christ's removing our sins through baptism in His name and giving us a robe of righteousness. Jesus Christ's blood from Calvary covers our blemishes, faults, imperfections, and badness, and when He looks at us, He sees only justified children. Joel's second chapter speaks of restoration and the removal of all shame.[53]

When we are restored, God will cause us to be at peace with ourselves and our past. The Lord will heal the wounds caused by our past and our shame, thus restoring us. Second Corinthians 12:9-10 reminds us that His grace is sufficient. Sufficient for everything that we tend to trip over. Sufficient for all the attributes and occasions we see through our shame-tinted lenses.

The final baby step is letting the Lord give us His peace. *Peace I leave with you, My peace I give unto you; not as the world gives do I give to you. Let not your heart be troubled, neither let it be afraid* (John 14:27, NKJV). In *Strong's Concordance, peace* means rest or quietness. The root word for *peace* means "to join something." This lets us know that something was broken and needs joined again. So wholeness is a product of restoration. This wholeness, or peace, is a result of the work of righteousness or being made at peace with your past, being healed, and being declared innocent.[54] Isaiah 32:17 and Philippians 3:7-9 give us tools to make peace with our past.

When these three baby steps are taken, joy will come to us. Joy and peace are possible in my life only after I have hope. Romans 15:13 promises us that the God of hope will fill us with joy and hope through the power of the Holy Ghost. Righteousness, peace, and joy are not human emotions. They are spiritual blessings from God and are produced by Him alone.[55]

This is the work of the Spirit in us once we escape the swamp and the toxic soundtracks of our minds. Right now, I declare peace, hope, and joy over you as you continue to take the baby steps necessary to escape the clutches of shame.

Jesus wants us to:

Allow ourselves to be broken and contrite in His presence.

Accept His love unconditionally.

Realize that God's mercy does endure and lasts forever.

Forgive ourselves of the grudge of shame.

Let Him make us whole in His image.

Let Him clothe us with His righteousness.

Help us fulfill His purpose in our lives![56]

Pray the Word over Your Mind

Your blood was shed for me at Calvary so that I could experience freedom from my sins and my shame. You, God, were beaten at the whipping post so that

I could be healed by Your stripes and have life more abundantly. You took on pain and suffering so that I may live my life free in You but only under Your blood and only through Your grace and mercy that is never-ending.

I am free from every stronghold I have erected in my mind because You are my Prince of Peace. Today, my mind and spirit are held in peace. Your peace comes only from Your presence, and I know You are here with me. You are my healer. You are Jehovah-Rophi.

I accept Your blood and the atoning power of that blood in my body today, for that blood heals and covers all my wrongs and trespasses. You said in Leviticus 17:11 that life is in the blood. The blood of sacrifice is for our redemption or atonement. John 6:53-58 tells me that I must partake of Jesus' blood and His body to bring His life into my death. I plead the blood over my mind and my life. I plead the blood of Jesus Christ as it's my only counteragent. Where there is no blood covering, sin is free to corrupt and destroy.

Today, I am comforted by the fact that the enemy cannot cross the bloodline of Jesus Christ. Hide me under Your blood and keep me from all willful sin and toxic thinking. Forgive me of my sins, my wickedness, and my evil desires to step outside Your law. Only through the new birth am I invited to eat the bread of life as my daily sustenance and know that Your blood cleanses me from all sin. Today, I remember the life of Jesus and His blood that He shed for me so that I may receive eternal life through God.

I close this chapter on atonement with the lyrics of an old hymn. Rev. G. T. Haywood, a pastor in Indianapolis, Indiana, wrote "I See a Crimson Stream of Blood" in 1920. I would love for you to find and listen to the hymn as you seek the Lord about His atoning power.

Remember that the life is in the blood! Your life is dependent upon your revelation of the blood of Jesus Christ, which He shed so freely for you.

1. On Calv'ry's hill of sorrow
Where sin's demands were paid,
And rays of hope for tomorrow
Across our paths were laid.

2. Today no condemnation
Abides to turn away
My soul from His salvation,
He's in my heart to stay.

3. When gloom and sadness whisper
You've sinned, no use to pray,
I look away to Jesus,
And He tells me to say:

4. And when we reach the portal
Where life forever reigns,
The ransomed host's grand final,
Will be this glad refrain.

Refrain
I see a crimson stream of blood.
It flows from Calvary,
Its waves which reach the throne of God,
Are sweeping over me.[57]

Reflection

1. Do you feel better or worse after this chapter? Why or why not?
2. Have you ever considered atonement as presented here?
3. How will this chapter change you?
4. What continues to trip you from behind?
5. Journal your thoughts or understanding of atonement. Yes, please. Even if you have been a Christian for 157 years.

Perfection God's Way

I wish I'd spent more time marinating in the luxury of being alive. I wish I hadn't taken for granted the cloudy days that invited me to stay present and just be. Sunny days are great, but it's the cloudy days, the quiet days, that bring you to your knees and ask you to see beneath the layers of your daily reality. These days are humble, and they're kind. They ask you to take a breath until you realize you've been holding one in for quite some time."
—Sonya Matejko[58]

Perfection. The absolute worst part of shame. It overtakes the best of us. Of course, we all want to put our best foot forward with anything we try to achieve for the kingdom and just life in general. The perfection I am talking about right now is intense and never-ending. It is way beyond just "wanting our best for God." Sure, we all say that when we're trapped in its vortex and can't figure out how to break free, but there's a better way.

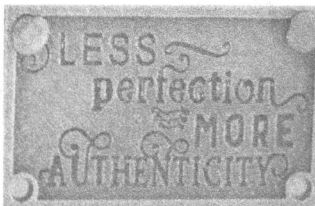

Yeah, I said it. Let's dive right into the dirty swamp and talk about perfection since it has a death grip on most people dealing with shame. Sadly, they are mostly unaware.

Anna Quindlen said about perfection, "The thing that is really hard, and really amazing, is giving up on being perfect and beginning the work of becoming yourself."

Brené Brown observes, "Where perfectionism exists, shame is always lurking. Shame is the birthplace of perfectionism. Perfection is,

129

at its core, about trying to earn approval and acceptance. Healthy striving is self-focused—How can I improve? Perfectionism is other-focused—What will they think?"

Her definition of perfectionism is a self-destructive and addictive belief system that fuels this primary thought: If I look perfect, live perfectly, and do everything perfectly, I can avoid or minimize the painful feelings of shame, judgment, and blame. It is self-destructive simply because there is no such thing as perfect. Perfection is an unattainable goal.

We want to be perceived as perfect, but there is no way to control the perception of others, regardless of how much energy and time we spend trying. Perfectionism is addictive because when we invariably experience shame, judgment, and blame, we usually believe it's because we weren't perfect enough. So rather than questioning the faulty logic of perfectionism, we become even more entrenched in our quest to live, look, and do everything just right.

Perfectionism never happens in a vacuum. It touches everyone around us. We pass it down to our children, we infect the workplace [and local churches, districts, and committees] with impossible expectations, and it's suffocating to our friends and families.[59]

How do we stop the madness of this crazy addictive behavior and begin to embrace healthy living with wholeheartedness? We do not have to remain in the kind of living where we freak out when friends make a surprise visit to our house. The kind of living where we run and hide, stop eating, or hate ourselves one more time when we cannot find anything to wear for that next conference. The kind of living where we refuse to allow anyone to help us decorate for the next season at the church at the office or at the house. Why do we think we have to live this way?

Remember that perfection and control are first cousins, and they love to hang out as often as possible! When we can control things, we can be perfect. When we allow others to help us, things begin to slip precariously out of control—our control—and we can't stand it. That is why perfectionists cannot bear to delegate or allow people into their tightly knit bubble to help in any way, even their own children.

I have a family member whose father never allowed them to play with the train that went around the Christmas tree. Why not? The kids might mess it up. I am sure we all know people who refuse to allow anyone to load their dishwashers for them. I could go on and on here. Why do I recognize this? Because I was that person: a controlling perfectionist who was never good enough to make myself feel better about myself.

Is God pleased with this behavior? Does the Word speak to this behavior? Does the Bible say, "Thou shalt not be a perfectionist?" Is perfection a continuum, and sometimes we're okay and other times we're really not okay? Does perfectionism lead to other things like offense if someone doesn't understand us? Or if other people become offended because of our toxic attitude and controlling behavior? Does all that sound godly or like Christ?

So how do we escape this faulty soundtrack and replace it with something better? Romans 8:15-39 explains that everything happens for our good. It insists that nothing, no thing, has the power to separate us from the love of God. Take a minute to read that passage and underline some verses that speak to you.

A revelation of the love of God was necessary in my life. John 15 made me realize my only job is to abide in Christ and in His love, and then most everything will work out. When our souls are in charge of us, we usually think that we will power through anything in life with enough grit and high-powered strength. Verses 3 and 5 were enlightening to me. I was made clean because of the word that Jesus spoke. Therefore, my assignment is to abide in Him and bear fruit since I can do nothing without Him.

Grace Offerings

"A moment of self-compassion can change your entire day. A string of such moments can change the course of your life" (Christopher K. Germer).

Dr. Kristin Neff is a researcher and professor and leads a self-compassion research lab in Houston, Texas, where she studies how to

131

develop and practice self-compassion. She says there are three elements to self-compassion: self-kindness, common humanity, and mindfulness. When we're kind to ourselves, we create a reservoir of compassion that we can extend to others. Our children learn to be compassionate watching us, and the people around us feel free to be authentic and connected.[60]

At first, self-compassion is difficult. When shame covers us, grace and compassion are completely foreign concepts. We are not good at either. But the time has come for us to learn this. This clunky consciousness is called grace and compassion. We can do this fine for others, but I am trying to say that you must learn this for yourself.

One way to offer yourself grace is to practice saying, "I am good. I am working to be better." Something quick and fast like, "God loves me, so I will love myself." You must do anything you can to hear yourself speaking these reframing words out loud.

"Replace your judgments with empathy, upgrade your complaining to gratitude, and trade in your fear for love."

Authenticity

There is no fear in love, but perfect love casts out fear, because fear involves punishment [torment], and the ones who fears is not perfected in love (I John 4:18, NASB).

This verse and the other passages of Scripture like this baffled my mind for a long time. I couldn't seem to figure out how not to fear and how love and fear were connected. One day as I prayed and read the Word, I finally realized that the love of God has no torment. If my mind was actively being tormented, that wasn't the love of God at work; instead, that was fear. I know, simple stuff here that God had to show me elementary school style.

What is authenticity? What is the opposite of authenticity? Brené Brown has an opinion that authenticity is not a trait, something we have or don't have. Rather, authenticity is a practice. It is an intentional choice of how we choose to live. It is a collection of choices we make every day. It is how we show up and choose to be our real selves, not covered and unrecognizable from all the swamp monsters. Authenticity is truly letting go of what other people think—or what you think they think—about how you live.

When we live in authentic ways, we make a decision to live imperfectly. Authentic living is when we struggle with being our real selves and are open to discussing that struggle with our safe groups of friends, our tribe. As we struggle and grapple with living free from shame and all its evil cousins, we make a conscious choice to invite grace, joy, and gratitude into our daily lives.

To answer the question, the opposite of authenticity is perfection. Someone gifted me with the tiny bronze sign at the beginning of this chapter. As I placed it on the wall near the garage exit, I purposefully hung it crooked. I wanted a tangible reminder to live as an authentic human who isn't bound to perfectionism anymore.

I will be honest. There are times when perfectionism sneaks back into my daily choices. Those times usually happen when I am serving and other people are involved; for example, as I create hospitality baskets for visiting speakers who travel into our state or when I serve food. I had so many ingrained toxic practices that I still must practice self-compassion and grace for myself.

When I find myself slipping back into toxic behavior, I tell people that I am a recovering perfectionist so I can hear myself speak those words. The next time you feel yourself lapsing into perfectionism, try saying those words out loud: "I am a recovering perfectionist." I know it feels clunky, weird, and unnatural, but we have to kick our minds into gear forcibly with some positively spoken words.

One year around the beginning of autumn, I managed to do something I never thought possible in all my years as a pastor's wife. I asked a new convert to hustle all the fall tubs out of the storage room and decorate for fall. Then, I did something even more unthinkable. I left town to head to the General Conference.

She was terrified at my request and asked, "What if you don't like what I do?"

I responded, "Whatever you do will be just fine!" I truly meant the words, too. On my way out of the church that evening, I told myself,

I will not redo anything when I return to town next weekend. I will not gripe or complain about anything she does. She is doing me a huge favor and I will love whatever she does.

And I did just that. Of course, she didn't decorate for fall like I would have decorated for fall. But that is the point. She decorated for fall, and I didn't have to. I had conquered two evil beasts from the swamp that season: perfectionism and control.

Thereafter, I can't say I have been perfect for everything involving decor or hospitality at the church or on the campground, but I have worked to improve every time I feel that urge to control and be perfect. For far too long, I railed against myself for any failings. At last, I have learned to release any failure or sense of not meeting God's measurements. We must learn to bring all of us to God and to each other, without shame and without running away for a few days.

In our search and pathway to authenticity, we must conquer the inner monsters that tell us not to vocalize our need for authenticity and connection with a safe community. This sounds crazy, but the minute you attempt to practice authenticity, other people will start to push back on you. Your actions make them nervous, and they feel convicted. We have all been taught to suppress bad feelings, and in doing so, many times, we have brought harm to our bodies and souls.

Shauna Niequist says that most of us have become soldiers instead of brothers and sisters or daughters and sons. We must adddress this frightening awareness. Authenticity is new territory. When we finally rally the gumption to leave the swamp of shame, we might fear the new normal. That is okay! As a matter of fact, you probably won't even know what is normal for a while. You will feel like a wobbly, newborn colt, but soon you will find your solid footing. Living with shame for a long time demands a long time to learn to live a different but better way.

Safe People

Boundaries must be learned and set for the toxic people in our lives—this includes ourselves. Many outward and inward expressions derive from the lack of boundaries in our lives. Dr. Henry Cloud believes that panic disorders fall into this category because people think they have no control over what happens to them. People feel out of control, and they must do whatever everyone wants them to do. No one is expected to give her life for the ministry, for her family, for her workplace, or for her boss.

> Doing and busyness were supposed to keep me safe, but instead they kept me numb. When you decide, finally, to stop running on the fuel of anxiety, desire to prove, fear, shame, and deep inadequacy—when you decide to walk away from that fuel for a while, there's nothing left except confusion and silence. You're on the side of the road, empty tank, no idea how to propel forward. It's disorienting, freeing, terrifying. For a while, you just sit, contendedly. Contentment is the most foreign concept you know. . . . You sit in your own skin, being just your own plain self. And it's okay. And it's changing everything.[61]

Boundary setting is important. In addition, identity is vital here. Dr. Cloud says, "If you know who you are in God, then you will also know what you feel, what you like, what you want, what you will do, and what you think." Defining these things is essential for your healing journey. "When you carve out an identity and say, 'This is who I am and who I am not,' then you begin to develop a 'no' muscle and will be able to set limits."[62]

Choosing values and practicing self-control are both important pieces of this link to setting boundaries. According to Stephen Covey in *Seven Habits of Highly Effective People*, figuring out your personal set of core values is one of the most revelatory things you can do as an exercise to figure out who you are and who you are not. The author states that the first habit that leads to effectiveness is learning to live proactively. I cannot say enough about this habit. Obviously, all seven habits are tremendously important, but if you implement only one habit this year, choose proactive living.

Dr. Henry Cloud identifies unsafe people as the critics, the irresponsibles, and the abandoners. These people avoid working on their problems instead of dealing with them. Unsafe people resist any form of character formation or growth usually because they are acting out their unconscious hurts and then hurting others. Unsafe people demand your respect instead of earning it, and they blame others instead of taking responsibility. They refuse to be in an authentic community with either friends or believers because they avoid closeness.

By the way, if you haven't already read the book, *Safe People*, by Dr. Henry Cloud, add it to your reading list for later.

I am spelling this out to help you identify unsafe people in your life once you begin your path to healing. If you continue to be sucked into the mud of the swamp by unhealthy behaviors, you can't get better without figuring out who and what continually drain your soul.

Dr. Cloud gives us a picture of a safe relationship: one that draws you closer to God, draws you close to others, and helps you become the real person God created you to be. As we move into healthy friendships and relationships, we first must be able to heal ourselves enough to withstand any backlash from the people we know. While this sounds crazy, there will be folks who are offended at your new realization and your new efforts to live shame-free. Why? As we said earlier, your new life of openness, brokenness, and healing will bring condemnation to them for their lack of all the above.

You have to draw your own spiritual and emotional property lines for the unsafe people in your life.[63] In doing so, you will experience freedom and love in a way that feels responsible and not harsh. Learning to be and live every day content as just plain ol' you will be more freeing than anything else. Stand strong and continue on your healing pathway no matter what anyone says or does. Learn to be inwardly strong for you. You matter!

Renewed Mind

Knowing that we all had (past tense) a broken relationship with God, others, and ourselves, we have hopefully developed some new behaviors that are both emotionally and spiritually sound. We still feel the emotional tugs to go back to shame, but we live past them in our relationship with our Creator. We must have a spiritual solution to repair all facets of our spirits, souls, and bodies.

The spiritual solution must be based on the love of God. God has wished for reconciliation with mankind since Genesis 3, and nothing is different now. We must be reconciled to God and His love.

The majority of doctors in traditional medicine focus only on symptoms and treat the symptoms with all sorts of medications. (Remember, this book is not dispensing medical advice, so talk to your doctor about any medications.) In functional medicine, doctors focus on the root of the problem to make the symptoms dissipate.

We must operate the same here. We cannot have superficial healing that is not lasting. Dr. Cloud says that when we resolve the issues, the symptoms will no longer have a reason to exist. The greatest attribute, says I Corinthians 13:13, is love. We must learn to be fully functioning human beings. In order to have a renewed mind, we must employ all three: spirit, soul, and body. God's love must be at the center of all we do, all we change, and all we strive for as we heal.

We must tackle our real versus our ideal selves. Dr. Cloud suggests that often the church at large stresses such high ideals that many people feel they cannot be human and still be Christian. They forget that they first came because they were sinners in need of forgiveness and acceptance by God.

Be careful and wary of any and all church traditions and cultures that are unhealthy. If it feels wonky, check your Word. It might be your newly found freedom that feels so strange, or it might be some weird stronghold in the form of a church tradition of extreme busyness or an ideal self mind-set that never is allowed to be human and have failures.

If we think of ourselves and others with a judgmental tone, we become condescending and full of wrath. When this happens, we judge ourselves right back into the shame swamp. If we are using any of these behaviors like shame, hiding, denial, splitting, and other defenses to hide the real us, we cannot accept God's grace in the long run. On the other hand, if we adopt a loving and accepting tone toward our real selves, there is hope for transformation. We must be able to accept all the pieces of ourselves that are not perfect. When that happens, we can move forward into healing and acceptance.[64]

We have many Scriptures about renewing our minds: Ephesians 4:23; Romans 8:5-6; 12:2; Philippians 4:7-8. Dr. Caroline Leaf has determined that it takes at least twenty-one days to build a long-term thought with its embedded memories and sixty-three days to make that into a habit. Thus, in order for you to have a renewed mind from shame and guilt and all the other swamp monsters, you will have to stick with this mind business for a long minute.

Check out the twenty-one-day mind detox from Dr. Caroline Leaf as it might help you build new mind muscles that you will need for the future. You can also study the next chapter, where I give my very elementary solution to renewing our minds. I elaborate on what I did as I was desperate to escape the shame vortex. Slowly, over time, my mind was renewed, and I was able to function as an authentic human for the first time.

Purpose

Purpose comes from the direction we prayerfully set for our lives. We must figure out what truth is for each of us. Disclaimer: When I say "truth" here, I do not mean doctrinal truth. That is absolute truth and never subjective truth to culture or what we presently feel to be right. I trust that your spiritual authority can point you in the right direction for doctrinal truth that is absolute. If not, email me, and we will chat.

Purpose comes after you have done the tough work of figuring out who you are in Christ and who you are as your real self. No more pretending here or being unrealistic. Every human has a kingdom purpose that is unlike any purpose for any other human.

I recently heard this hack to pinpoint your life purpose: If you were given unlimited money and a cleared calendar, what would you do? Also, if you could speak to every single person on the earth at the same time in one ginormous megaphone, what solution would you offer? What problem were you put on this earth to solve?

These questions are meant to be difficult. Discovering or redis-covering your purpose is going to seem very difficult for now, but as you pray, meditate on God's Word, and give yourself space and time, God will reveal His purpose for your life. I promise! For so long now, you have been stuck in the swamp, but you are out finally and getting the muck cleaned off.

Once you move from the swamp, you will begin to absorb the beautiful sights that surround you. Take the time to see them in depth. Find joy in the smallest things today. Your journey has been arduous and tough to this point, but now, you're moving into loving yourself for yourself through the grace and mercy of a God who never once left you alone.

Godly Confidence

There is a huge difference between godly confidence and arro-gance. As we move toward perfection God's way, we must learn to be confident in our authority and spiritual gifting. Living in shame will make you believe that you are flawed and never good enough to be a vessel in God's big kingdom. This is a lie from your enemy who wants to keep your head down and keep you in the swamp of lies.

Due to our prior habit of toxic thinking, we wrongly think that when we are free of shame, we might turn into annoyingly proud or arrogant people. If you practice brokenness from the earlier chapters, this will not happen. A haughty attitude simply isn't possible while we practice being broken before God in a healthy way.

Pride says, "God needs me. This church needs me, and they can-not make it without me. They could not do XYZ without me. I am needed. I am the most talented, so I am the only person for the job."

Godly confidence acknowledges, "Without God, I can do abso-lutely nothing. I have submitted to the pain and brokenness in my life and have pulled the pain close enough to consume the flesh from my heart and my soul. I have complete dependence upon God."

Once we get to this place, not one person is able to hurt us anymore. Why not? Our souls are completely dependent upon God. They are healed, so as we walk in godly authority, we are full of humility, love, and total absence of fear. We are vulnerable and are open books to the world. We harbor no secrets and no darkness in which to hide stuff from the swamp.

God's Love

To love the way that God would have us love, we must be willing to pivot our toxic thinking. The way I feel about myself matters. My capacity to love myself affects my ability to love God and others. If I believe I am unlovable, I will refuse to allow God to love me. If I convince myself that I am not worthy of God's love, I will reject His love. Therefore, I become unloved.

God will not and cannot love me against my will. In addition, if I feel unloved by God, I cannot possibly love anyone else. Remember my story? I was incapable of demonstrating love to Rick or anyone else because I felt unloved by my God. *We know love by this, that He laid down His life for us; and we ought to lay down our lives for the brethren* (I John 3:16, NASB).

God's love is the conduit through which all His blessings flow to us. If we do not allow Him to love us unconditionally, He cannot save or heal us, supply our needs, or answer our prayers. We simply cannot make our self-esteem better by thinking a certain way. For years, shame has prevented you from hearing, believing, or living the truth of God's love for you just as you are.

> God loves us because of who we are and not because of what we do. —Chester Wright

Write these next two phrases on a card and memorize this truth: I cannot be good enough for God to love me more. I cannot be bad enough for God to love me less.

I first heard that from an elder in my husband's home church in Oklahoma City. It rocked my world, for I was raised to believe the opposite. My capacity for loving others is severely diminished when I do not love myself.

Loving others is fundamental to harvest. My inability for God to love me hinders His ability to love others through me, which raises a huge roadblock to harvest. If you have struggled to teach Bible studies or to participate in outreach, there's your answer. Again, you are not flawed. You had shame. You are now aware and working through the shame, and healing will come.

A revelation of the love of God, just like the blood of Christ in the earlier chapter on atonement, is the key to your understanding. Make this a matter of prayer. Read and memorize every verse you can locate about the love of God. Start in I John like I did. Write your name in the pronouns so you can hear yourself saying the Scriptures to yourself with your name in them.

Two-thirds Responsibility

Spirit, soul, and body—those are the three aspects we introduced to start this book. *Now may the God of peace himself sanctify you completely; and may your whole spirit, soul, and body be preserved blameless at the coming of our Lord Jesus* (I Thessalonians 5:23, NKJV). The Lord has given us the responsibility of two-thirds of the whole: soul and body. We are the owners of our souls and the guardians of our bodies. If the Lord has entrusted the two to our care, we must figure out the optimal way to maintain both.

Hebrews 4:12 tells us that *the word of God is living and powerful, and sharper than any two-edged sword, piercing even to the division of soul and spirit, and of joints and of marrow, and is a discerner of the thoughts and intents of the heart* (NKJV). The Word of God is the only thing powerful enough to cut between our soul and our spirit, as well as know what we think and intend to do.

In order to make God greater in us, we must make ourselves less through crucifying our souls, or our flesh, so that God may speak to us. We must take up our crosses and deny our human spirits, our souls, and follow hard after God every day. (See Luke 9:23.)

We must close all open gateways in the soul: rebellion, unbelief, grudges, unforgiveness, pride, arrogance, Jezebel, Absalom, and any other access to unholy influences. Then, we can be truly like Christ and hear his voice. We simply cannot afford to live separated from God. Every day, make sure your spirit is in sync with your Creator.

Community of Believers

Psalm 68:6 likens the church to a family. The Lord's plan was not for us to do life alone in a silo. We are supposed to be connected as a body of believers in covenant together. Once we have been baptized into the blood of Christ, we are connected through the covenant. The Lord takes covenantal relationships quite seriously.

Paul taught in I Corinthians 12:12-22 that we are all members of the body of Christ. Romans 12:4-5 explains that the church is one body consisting of many members.

One reason the Lord created the church was for us to have a safe place to grow. Members of the body of Christ are brothers and sisters. We are all siblings in God's great family. When we interact with each other, the Lord allows our interactions to perfect us in His love. Just as my natural siblings and I have disagreements and upsets and differences, so does the body of Christ. We learn how to love God, love others, and love ourselves at church while connected to the body of Christ, our family.

We must agree to suffer for each other's perfection. This is perfection God's way. We must be able to bond with people as well as establish emotional attachments to others in order to share thoughts, dreams, and feelings among ourselves. We must become emotionally and soul-healthy enough to do this and be safe enough that people may trust us. If we cannot trust the body of Christ, we are in trouble!

Our souls grow by being connected to each other. Therefore, we cannot prosper properly without a healthy community and connection. Biblical humility recognizes our dependence on God and on other people. We should no longer think we are warriors fighting alone or martyrs standing in a solitary post.

Through many years, I had trouble recognizing that I needed the body of Christ. My soul wanted to be self-sufficient and do things on my own. After my dad died, I wanted merely to come to church and slip out the side door without having to talk to anyone. I didn't want an attachment to anyone. I was deeply hurt and mistakenly thought I could make it alone. In my stubbornness and self-centeredness, I pushed away the body. I rejected the one resource that could have brought me into a community to grieve with me.

Nothing grows anywhere in God's universe apart from the course of strength and nutrition. John 15 establishes the rule of abiding. In this chapter, we find that without connection to others and God, we slowly wither and die. The branch, when disconnected from the tree, dies alone. Likewise, when we step away from the body of Christ, we will shrivel and die alone.

God's nature in the church manifests bonding—to Himself and to those in His body. When we embrace vulnerability and healing through relationships, we expose our shame and scarcity that allege we are never enough. To be truly perfect in God's kingdom, we must have relationships. We must be attached to God and others, for without those links, we simply cannot be our true selves.

Failures Are Not Final

R. D. Whalen noted that a perfect child cries, stumbles, messes his diaper, and makes messes. That's what perfect children do. Thus, it should come as no surprise that a perfect child of God sins, fails, falls, trespasses, and makes big, messy mistakes. We are not perfect gods; we are perfect children of God.

That perfect God created perfect children with a capacity for making mistakes. Consequently, children make mistakes because that's what children do. *My little children, these things I write unto you, so that you may not sin. But if anyone does sin, we have an advocate with the Father* (I John 2:1, NKJV).

We lack grace for each other, especially for those in the household of faith. Why is this so difficult? Psalm 103:14 reminds us, *He knows our frame; He remembers that we are dust* (NKJV). We are too hard on ourselves and others. My family has an adage that fits well here: We judge others by their actions but ourselves by our intentions.

When was the last time you heard of a failure, a public exposé of a minister or a recognized figure, and your first thought was, *How will we restore that person?* Somehow, we get all wrapped up in the gory details of said failure and seem to forget that he or she was a perfect child of God who sinned. Romans 3:23 reminds us that we have all sinned and come short of the glory of God.

The next time you fail, celebrate because you are a perfect child whom God loves and forgives the instant you ask. Hannah Brencher posted a blog:

> Promise me you'll fail. . . . Promise me that. Promise me you'll stumble. You'll make mistakes—big ones and little ones. You'll be unafraid to ask questions. Promise me you won't let fear drive the car. You will explore possibilities, you will partner with yourself instead of bullying yourself. You will mess things up. You will try your best. You will be unafraid of the doors that slam in your face again and again. You will bearhug rejection. You will cheer on the victories of others. You won't let people belittle your creativity. You will refuse to be kicked down by the things in this world that want to yell in your face, "You can't. You shouldn't. You won't." You will silence the loud and rowdy naysayers with one footstep after another footstep. You will give yourself grace. Buckets of grace. Promise me you'll fail. Failure is one of the sweetest parts of this life thing. It will mold you. It will make you new. It will push you to be better tomorrow than you were yesterday. Promise to fail and try, and mess up, and give yourself and others grace. Big, big, grace.

Reflection

At a ladies' conference a few years back, I heard Rachel Coltharp ask these four questions:

1. How much do I want to be separated unto God for a holy purpose?
2. How peaceful do I want to be?
3. How blessed do I want to be?
4. How obedient do I want to be?

In light of those questions and this chapter:

1. How will you get to that place of humility where all of you (soul: feel, want, think) is gone and only Jesus is left?
2. How will you be perfect God's way?
3. What baby steps will you take this week for perfection done God's way?

The Daily's

Ⅰt's the little daily changes that cumulatively make the biggest difference."
                                        —Dr. Caroline Leaf

"Everyone buys books, but few ever read them. Everyone wants growth, but few accept pain. Everyone wants to be happier, but few ever change. Intention is nothing without action, but action is nothing without intention" (The Growing Investor, Instagram).

God Connection

This term was coined by Terry and Melani Shock from Kingdom Quest Ministries. They have a daily devotion for purchase on their website that has each of the components of a daily God Connection. If you do not have a system in place that works for you, you could give their system a go. God Connection is simply your daily, consistent time with the Lord that encompasses prayer, gratitude, thanksgiving, the Word, meditation, and Scripture memory. Through their teaching, we have learned not to separate the pieces into clunky parts but rather to appreciate everything together as one whole package.

It took me years upon years to find a good system that worked for me. Now, I have a system that is a hybrid of the Shocks' method. I use a disc-bound notebook system with daily prayer pages in a binder that travels with me. When that binder gets too full, I simply remove the sheets from the past few weeks and add them to the current year's disc-bound notebook.

Again, you must find what works for you. I have a cabinet full of moleskin notebooks I have kept over the years. I have retained notes from sermons over decades. With the inspiration of Melani's daily process, I finally found a system that works for me. Just having a system will silence the chatter in your head about your lack of prayer time, Bible time, and so on.

I have found that a consistent place for a God Connection is also quite important. I have a prayer chair where I normally sit to write my daily prayer page. In addition, I have found that I love to pray while walking along the country roads where I currently live. Then, after I have walked my mile or so, I come back to the house to finish my prayer page.

I sometimes use the back of my prayer page to take sermon notes, jot grocery lists, glue in fun mementos from trips, and dabble in all things paper. My daily prayer page disc-bound notebook doubles as my planner and keeper of all the trappings of the voyage. I also have crafted a prayer book that is part scrapbooked prayer pages and part lists of things I pray about, including prayer guides I have created over the years.

When considering your God Connection time, the most important factor is that you pray until you feel and sense the peace of God. This might come as you pray or as you read your Word. Your daily connection with God is the most important piece of this entire chapter. Figure out how to make it work for you consistently.

Another element I learned from the Shocks is the principle of the first filter. This simply means that we must put the Word of God before anything else in our day. No texts. No news. No weather. No conversation if possible. And, for crying out loud, no social media before you read the Word of God.

I make this work by having an audio Bible plan (YouVersion). As soon as I awaken, I listen to my chapters of that daily plan. I listen as I get dressed. I have trained my mind to hear the Word of God first.

Many of you, upon hearing this, reply, "Oh, I can't listen to the Bible on audio because I miss stuff." "Does listening to the Bible really count?" "What if I miss an entire section?"

I respond in turn: Calm down. Take a chill pill. You are being self-righteous about something that is purely God's Word, designed to bring us peace and direction. Yes, I will also read an actual Bible later as I mentioned above. I have a bookmark system that I use for reading ten chapters a day. If I don't get to all ten chapters or all of my audio Bible in a day, I offer myself grace just like I hope you would give me grace for missing a text from you.

After many, many conversations about people's fear of missing or not doing their daily Bible reading quite right, I have realized that we are far too pharisaical and driven by perfection concerning our time with the Lord. The point is our relationship with our Creator. He does not stand with a stopwatch and a daily chore chart to make sure we read X number of chapters and pray Z number of minutes.

If you read the same chapter for ten weeks in a row, that is fine! Actually, that is wonderful. You will glean so much! If you somehow sleep through your alarm and miss all of your God Connection for a day or even two, good grief, please, give yourself the gift of grace and self-compassion. Everything will be okay. I promise. If nothing else, you have provided yourself an excellent opportunity to practice self-love and authentic living.

Affirmations and Systems

One book I found exceptionally helpful is *The Miracle Morning* by Hal Elrod. The author offers a simple plan for mornings and beats the mind monsters at their own game with consistency and intentionality. The schedule he offers for each morning doesn't work for me, but his affirmation system was illuminating.

I sound a warning bell here to be on the lookout for humanistic fixes and solutions to tell you to make yourself better with words and all sorts of craziness. That is not what we are about. We will combat and heal from shame with the Word of God and by the atoning power of the blood of Jesus Christ!

While we will use words, we will approach healing each day from the lens of the Word. Ann Voskamp observes, "Without the lens of the Word, the world warps." Our minds and hearts will warp if we embrace healing from any source other than God and His Word.

Muhammad Ali remarked, "It's the repetition of affirmations that leads to belief. Once that belief becomes a deep conviction, things begin to happen." His words are so true. Once you embark on a daily practice of affirmations, you will be hooked, I hope!

We have all been in the terrible practice of repeating toxic things to ourselves each day, so now we will flip that script and begin to speak faith and declare our purpose and healing. Hal Elrod reported that "80 percent of women have self-deprecating thoughts about themselves (body image, job performance, others' opinions of them, etc.)." Your affirmations work either for or against you, depending on how you use them.

If you don't purposefully and carefully design the affirmations with your purpose and healing in mind,

> You are susceptible to repeating and reliving fears, insecurities, and limitations of your past. So writing your affirmations must be in alignment with what you want to accomplish and who you need to be to accomplish it. You must commit to repeating them daily (ideally out loud) and they immediately make an impression on your subconscious. Your affirmations will work to transform the way you think and feel so that you may overcome your limiting beliefs and behaviors and replace them with those you need to succeed.[65]

Other books to consider for learning about daily affirmations are *Think and Grow Rich* by Napoleon Hill and *The Traveler's Gift* by Andy Andrews.

When I started to write my personal affirmations, I employed his system. Elrod has a five-step system for creating affirmations.

Step one is what you really want in life. This entails your beliefs, attitudes, and habits, so your affirmations must clearly focus on improving all areas of your life. To begin, you must spend time in prayer and the Word to hear God speak to you regarding your goals, beliefs, and His plan to be fulfilled in your life. Again, this is all new to your mind, so don't get overwhelmed at first. Take it slow. Give it time. Don't forget baby steps for moving forward.

Step two is the why. Why do you want what you listed in step one? At this juncture, you need to stop and clearly define your life purpose. I will offer some resources in the appendix to assist with this; however, the only person who can determine this is you! You cannot read it in a book or see it on your phone screen. Your spouse cannot tell you what your life purpose is. Nope. Gotta dig down deep in that newly formed foundation of yours and figure it out.

Step three is "Do does not equal Be." You must be who you are before you can do. For your entire life, you have lived opposite to this. You have grown so accustomed to doing to be that you might struggle a lot with being first and then doing. How do you just "be"? Living and just "being" takes getting used to, for sure!

One way to find this state is to slow down. *Redeeming Your Time* by Jordan Raynor is a great volume that helps with "being" first. Another great read is *Present over Perfect* by Shauna Niequist. This book completely changed me. I highly recommend that you find a copy to own. I know. When people make the statement that such and such has completely changed them, I am always dubious. But I have read that book at least five times and listened to the audiobook even more frequently than that. I make it a habit to revisit Niequist's book every year to keep myself on track with "being" first and continuing the work of living authentically.

Step four are the actions that your affirmation will need to see it achieved, the application needed to get the work checked off the list. This step was nebulous in Elrod's book, but I think he meant we should do whatever possible to make the affirmation come to pass. Put life processes in place to ensure that you make room for the affirmation to occur.

Step five is continually adding motivational quotes, Scriptures, and various encouragement items to your ever-growing collection of your healing journey items, your ephemera of all the joyful things, and bits of this and that.

As you create your daily affirmations, don't get caught up in perfection. You will update and refine them many times as you grow and heal through the words. The first affirmations I created are extinct. That version of me simply does not exist anymore. The Lord has lifted me to new places and new stages of my healing journey. This doesn't mean that I am not myself; rather, it means that I have grown. Some of the words need constant upkeep to keep up with my healing.

An example of daily affirmations from my prayer book:

- ✦ I am 100 percent committed to spending time with the God of heaven to download His plan for today and my future.
- ✦ I will simply gather the manna that He has sent for today.
- ✦ I will not fret about yesterday or tomorrow.
- ✦ Today, I will live in the overflow of everything God allows through His Spirit and His Word.
- ✦ I will seek to leave a residue of His love and power on every person I interact with today.
- ✦ I have allowed myself to be free of perfectionism and control.
- ✦ I seek to rumble with vulnerability.
- ✦ I seek to add value to others' lives through daily demonstrations of love, grace, and mercy.
- ✦ I will speak with authenticity and honesty. Some will judge me, criticize me, and talk about me while others will honor, respect, and spread goodwill about me while earnestly praying for my continued prosperous journey through this life. Everyone who truly knows me will appreciate that I am both honest and transparent.
- ✦ I seek to add value to the lives of those around me through love and sincere reflection.

Word Replacement Therapy

When we have shame and toxic thoughts, we tend to give ourselves hate speech instead of grace. If we treated anyone else like we treat ourselves most days, we most likely wouldn't have a single friend or family left within a fifty-mile radius. Obviously, we want to treat everyone around us fairly and with love as the New Testament commands us. But how to make that switch?

Hopefully, you didn't skim over the last chapter about rewiring your brain and your mind. Your mind has to be rewired with new neural pathways. The only way to create new pathways is the Word.

Years ago, I learned a term from a dear elder, Claudette Walker. She coined the term *Word replacement therapy*. You can listen to her testimony on YouTube as she explains how she learned to replace her toxic thoughts that were straight-up lies from the enemy by using Scripture. Basically, every thought that is not based on the truth of the Word of God has to be systematically replaced over time with Scriptures that speak the opposite to the lies. Claudette asked God to show her how to rewire her mind, and over time, God showed her a verse to refute every single lie she had believed.

(Claudette's YouTube channel is titled *Open Hearts*. One message in which she shares this testimony about the replacement of thoughts with Scripture is the *Awakened* Friday morning service from The Church Triumphant in Pasadena, Texas.)

To make this happen in my life, I simply began by purchasing a ring of small index cards from Wal-Mart. I wrote verses of Scriptures on the cards and carried the ring everywhere I went. Dentist. School. Trips. Home. Sectional rallies. Everywhere. It became my survival weapon. We already know that II Corinthians 10:4-5 counsels us to destroy *every lofty [or toxic] thing raised up against the knowledge of God, and we are [to take] every thought captive to the obedience of Christ* (NASB). The cards offered a way to apply that passage.

Once again, big sigh, incongruence. We know this in our subconscious mind but do not always actively pursue what the Scriptures teach us to do in everyday life. The Word commands us to destroy every toxic thought that is a lie against the nature and authority of God. Your mind is the best computer on the face of the earth. When you feel stress or tension, your mind tells you how to respond. In time, this becomes a stronghold. Over time, these strongholds in our minds dictate to us how we will think, which then tell our emotions what to feel and our will to decide what it wants. The suggestions and demands are all your mind directing you on how you will respond to everything that happens to you.

The only way to change this process is through Word replacement therapy. Replace each and every thought that comes from the stronghold with Scripture. To tear down the strongholds, we must stop feeding our emotions and listening to the thoughts that come from our subconscious minds.[66] We find the roadmap in II Corinthians 10:3-5 for tearing down the strongholds in our minds.

In *Christians and Strongholds: Breaking Free and Staying Free from Internal Captivity*, Kim Haney explains, "Strongholds are built in our minds when we harbor and protect toxic thoughts which lead to bondage and heaviness. . . . A stronghold is a place or a point of operation where Satan is able to keep Christians captive in their minds. His lies are masked with logic." She added, "In order for us to maintain the healing and stay delivered from these oppressive forces, we have to continually apply the Word of God and challenge our thoughts by verbally speaking the Word of God when they come around." To that, I say, "Amen!"

To make this happen, we must be willing to play the long game. This process will not and logically cannot happen overnight. Once again, we all wish it would happen in a blinding flash of Holy Ghost inspiration at an altar service. I am not saying God can't do that, for He can do anything! But, once again, the long game. If you're willing to play the long game with this, your mind will be free, but you have to work at every thought. Every. Single. Thought. That. You. Think.

Examples of Word replacement therapy from my prayer book:

+ I am the body of Christ. Satan has no power over me because I overcome evil with good (I Corinthians 12:27; Romans 12:21).
+ I will fear no evil, for You are with me, Lord. Your Word and Your Spirit comfort me (Psalm 23:4).
+ Christ has redeemed me from the curse of the law. Therefore, I forbid any sickness or disease to come upon this body. Every

disease, germ, and virus that touches this body dies instantly in the name of Jesus. Every organ and every tissue of this body will function in the perfection in which God created it to function, and I forbid any malfunction in this body, in the name of Jesus (Galatians 3:13; Romans 8:11; Genesis 1:31; Matthew 16:19).

✦ No weapon formed against me shall prosper, for my righteousness is of the Lord. But whatever I do will prosper, for I am like a tree that's planted by the rivers of water (Isaiah 54:17; Psalm 1:3).

You are capable of formulating this exact defense for your own benefit. On our Kingdom Advance website, a set of Scripture cards is available for purchase. I offer a coupon here for 20 percent off—discount code *Journey*—if you would like to utilize the cards already designed for your devices. These cards will assist you in replacing toxic thoughts with Scripture and Word replacement therapy.

But all you really need is your Bible and a pen, perhaps a concordance (digital or otherwise). Get creative. Use markers and washi tape, my favorite thing to do with my prayer book!

Exercise and Sleep

Dr. Caroline Leaf discusses food, exercise, and sleep in her book, *Think and Eat Yourself Smart: A Neuroscientific Approach to a Sharper Mind and Healthier Life*. She alludes to the fact that we simply cannot think healthy thoughts without sleep, and we cannot properly digest the food we eat without sleep. Lack of sleep impairs higher-order thinking and self-control.

God expects us to guard our minds, souls, and bodies. Nevertheless, we seem to think that we can do anything we want to our bodies, and then we find ourselves frustrated when our bodies begin to break down. When we regularly do not get enough sleep, our endocrine system gets out of whack. That leads to overeating. Combine overeating with eating late in the evening, and our sleep is limited due to our busy lives. We do not achieve quality sleep when we do sleep, and the body becomes stressed.

Push yourself to gain an understanding of how a lack of sleep and poor sleep quality really do damage to our minds and bodies. Don't be one of those people who argue, "Sleep! We'll sleep when we're dead or in the nursing home!" That's completely ignorant and not at all good stewardship of the body God has given us to guard and keep.

Talk to a nutritionist or a functional doctor about the use of supplements and if you should be taking anything due to imbalances in your body. That is being proactive and taking care of ourselves, a new and scary venture as you journey out of the swamp. The new normal can be more scary than staying mired in the swamp!

Physical activity increases blood flow to our brains. Thus, our thoughts improve instantly with exercise. Not only do thoughts improve, but our memory is improved as well. Exercise and sleep help us move short-term memory to long-term memory. One of the most important things you can do to help your body is to get off your bottom several times each day. You can read research report after report that shows the danger of a sedentary lifestyle.

You don't even have to spend money on exercise. If you meet with someone to talk, grab a coffee or tea and head to a park to walk and talk. If you're just starting, walk for ten to fifteen minutes a day. Walk after a large meal. You could listen to your audio Bible as you walk. You could take advantage of audiobooks or podcasts. I enjoy walking and praying each morning.

Set a small but doable goal for daily steps for the next week. Figure out how many steps you take in fifteen minutes and simply create a goal for yourself for five days of the week.

Lymphatic System Drainage

Do you realize that our lymphatic systems drain only with movement or with exercise? The purpose of this book is not education for the health of our bodies, nor am I an expert on any of these things. However, I have studied and read extensively about our bodies' need

156

for movement to survive and thrive. Study your endocrine system, the effects of inflammation, and the drainage of the lymphatic system.

This is one of the major reasons we must exercise and move our bodies every day. We have any number of options: walking, jumping on a rebound trampoline, swimming, biking, and others.

We tell my eighty-six-year-old mother that motion is lotion. She even goes to a water exercise class several times a week and walks daily with her Nordic walking sticks for added balance. If she can do this, the rest of us have zero excuses!

Real Food

If our bodies are temples for the Holy Ghost, how are we treating them? Are we any different from the children of Israel, who polluted their land with worship to false gods and set up worship in the groves and the high places? Since being sick with chronic illness for years, I have been forced to examine the food that enters my body. I repeat, this book is not intended to be medical advice or to take the place of anything your medical professionals instruct you. This is only my journey and my story.

Food is medicine. The food we put in our bodies either makes us or breaks us. I submit no apologies for the worn-out clique. Not sorry! This is true.

Rachel Coltharp commented, "When we pull into McDonald's and ask God to bless the junk that we're about to partake of, are we sinning since we know it's all bad?"

Read about food from highly qualified people like your local nutritionists, Steven Gundry, Mark Hyman, and Dr. Caroline Leaf. Educate yourself on how you either bless or pollute your godly temple daily. I realize I am being possibly harsh, but we have to take a step back to look at our gluten, sugar, and caffeine intake. Since 2020 and my bout with COVID-19, I've been forced to switch to a gluten-free, corn-free, and mostly inflammatory food-free diet.

Figure out what is right for your body. If we are healing our minds, we also must address the healing of our bodies. They are not separate from each other as each has a strong impact on the other. While you might scoff at my eating habits, I am mostly free from the multiple symptoms I experienced after my sickness.

All I am imploring you to do is to educate yourself outside of Pinterest and Instagram about your food, namely sugar and caffeine.

Okay, everyone breathe. The rant is now over.

Sustained Change for Good

Researcher and writer Elisabeth Kübler-Ross noted, "People are like stained glass windows. They sparkle and shine when the sun is out, but when darkness sets in, their beauty is revealed only if there is light from within."

So what changes will you begin making for good? My best recommendation is that you choose small, daily baby steps at first. If you start with changes that are giant in scope, you will end up feeling worse about yourself and any changes you thought you were making. Ask me. I know about this. I have started many projects that were grandiose in scale and ended up in a heap such that my face—sliding along the dirty floor—looked like a kid pressed against the glass.

Brené Brown has a friend who makes herself accountable to herself daily. She speaks aloud questions formed from the acronym of the five-plus-one vowels: A, E, I, O, U, and Y.

A: Have I been Authentic today? (I changed this word to fit our use here.)

E: Have I Exercised today?

I: What have I done for myself today?

O: What have I done for Others today?

U: Am I holding Unexpressed shame/emotions today?

Y: Yeah! What is something good that happened today for which I am thankful?

You could simply put the vowels on a Post-it near your bathroom mirror or bedside table. When you see the letters, you can go through the questions quickly in your mind, but be sure to say the words out loud to yourself. This is the double imprint necessary for the mind to change and rewire the neurons.

How do we shine in the dark? We will only achieve sustained change for good with small, consistent, daily steps. Start by figuring out what you see yourself accomplishing in one month, in six months, and in one year.

Jon Acuff has a new book, *All It Takes is a Goal.* James Clear has written *Atomic Habits.* I recommend that you check out both books through the app *Libby* and your library card. Skim both books to see if their approaches would work for you.

Mantras

Create a phrase or two that will get you through the week. It might be a Scripture or a positive quote. While mantras are mostly associated with meditation, I feel that mantras are a way to combat stress, toxicity, and cortisol spikes.

If you recall the story about my drive to Florida in the summer of 2020, I scribbled a mantra onto the index card. It served as the boundary to which I forced my mind to submit while I drove with unsettling symptoms and an uncertain path ahead. Those words gave me something to focus on immediately when my crazy mind was trying to take over during those long days.

When you have your phrases or list of words, transfer them to a Post-it note or something you will be able to see throughout the day. Then, as your mind attempts to slide back into the murky swamp waters, forcibly command your mind to obey you. Just allow the mantra to do its work. Though this might sound crazy, at least try it for a day to see if it works for you.

As you heal, you will try and fail at many approaches. That is okay! Remember, failure is good. It means you are moving forward and falling forward. If you always have forward motion, even in a stumble, that still counts as progress. I still remind myself that I am working on progress—not perfection.

Journaling

Journaling is shown to be healing for both heart and mind. It might feel vulnerable to write things, stirring up memories and emotions that are tied to grief, toxic thought patterns, distorted thinking, and other negative results. If you are not accustomed to journaling your healing, you might look at *Ordering Your Private World* by Gordon MacDonald. The author offers a lot of great strategies for keeping a record of your thoughts as you heal from shame and you work on the rediscovery of your purpose.

Another journaling book is *Take Two: A Journal for New Beginnings*. My sister gifted this small book to me as we embarked on a new life after pastoring for thirty years. The prompts were really good and engaged my mind and heart as I wrote about the transition.

Psalm 23

The presence of the Lord brings restoration and healing. Before you go to sleep at night, quote Psalm 23 aloud. Marilyn Chennault was a strong believer in quoting Psalm 23 every day of our lives. She believed there was healing in that psalm.

As you quote it, meditate on the words about lying in green pastures and being led beside still waters. Sheep will not go to sleep if they are nervous, hungry, or afraid. We must give all fear to the Lord and realize that He is with us. Consequently, we have no reason to fear. Shadows cannot hurt us.

We walk through the valley of the shadow of death, but we don't stop. Two guardian angels—goodness and mercy—are always with us, in front and behind. I must have enough in my cup that I overflow in others' cups each day. I must live in the overflow of the goodness of God today and every day.

> If you can't fly, then run.
> If you can't run, then walk.
> If you can't walk, then crawl.

But whatever you do,
you have to keep moving forward.
—Dr. Martin Luther King, Jr.

Reflection

1. Journal five things that are your strengths.
2. Journal five things, only five, that are your weaknesses.
3. Now, journal how to turn the weaknesses into strengths. If that is too difficult, forget it for now. Really.
4. Write an exercise goal for the next week. Only one.
5. Write a goal for God Connection for the next week. One.
6. Write one way that you will work to cleanse your lymphatic system this week.
7. Begin to journal affirmations from Scripture. Write at least one affirmation about one area right now.
8. How will you begin Word replacement therapy?

See Your Way Out

"It's time to say goodbye, but I think goodbyes are sad and I'd much rather say hello. Hello to a new adventure."
—Ernie Harwell

When our son was a teenager, full of life and snark, he had a saying that made me crack up and mad at him, all at the same time. If he and I were having an intense conversation, otherwise known as a mother-son battle of the wills, he would make this remark if his dad thought to interject something into our discussion. "Dad, this is an A-B conversation, so C your way out!" I must add that this never ended well in our house.

That being said, all things need an ending. As some things end, other things begin. Your newly found journey out of the swamp has begun, which means your toxic thinking is coming to an end.

Through the chapter on the revelation, we educated ourselves about a troublesome situation in our inner beings, and we called it a swamp. We journeyed back to Genesis to figure out why we are prone to sin and impossible behavior.

Through the chapter about stolen identity, we read about roles versus our purpose. Here we began the renovation of our foundation. Some of us either have stolen or lost identities that we have worked to reclaim and rediscover through the pages of this book and those of the greatest book, the Bible.

Next, we took a journey into the murky waters of the swamp. Here we concluded that many of us have lost our compass and kingdom purpose as we ran hard after approval and exhibited other behaviors that are so unhealthy. Trauma and addiction to approval met us in the swamp as we battled for self-protection.

The soundtracks chapter had us renovating old tunes and figuring out new tunes to play in our minds. As we dug into our defense mechanisms and distorted thinking, we began to realize that the only way out of the swamp is through the creation of new pathways in the brain through neuroplasticity. One way to build new pathways is to realize who we are in Christ, which comes through His Word.

Atonement was a powerful chapter where we began to place our faith in God's Word once more as we received His love for us. We recognized afresh Jesus' supreme sacrifice that He paid at Calvary. Through a revelation of the great price paid at the cross, we can finally find wholeness and realize that Jesus Christ was broken so that we might have life and life abundant.

Perfection God's way is the understanding that we are only perfect through the grace of Jesus Christ. Through that daily dose of grace, we find authenticity and a renewed mind. We grasp that God doesn't see our failure as final. We learn to create boundaries to keep us and our close circle safe people while we begin the process of rediscovering our kingdom purpose.

In "The Daily's," the rubber meets the road. It's where we put down a stake and say, "Okay, right here, at this very spot, I begin my journey of baby steps toward healing and restoration." All the combined pieces—God Connection, affirmations, Word replacement therapy, exercise, and sleep—create sustained changes that over time will bring us great joy and peace that last. Don't forget to work to create your own kingdom affirmations through great books like *I Am 3: I Am Who the I Am Says I Am: The Power of Identity*, by Donavon Hill.

You might be curious how long the healing from shame lasts. All I can say is that healing will last as long as you put in the hours to create the change. When you become serious about your inner renovation to the foundation, you will find yourself taking slow but sure steps away from the swamp each day.

I have heard, "The days are long, but the years are short." That is how I think of healing from shame. You might have days that feel never-ending, yet in a couple of years, you will realize how far you have come.

As you make the journey from the swamp and into the sunshine, my sincere wish is that you continue the journey. Don't stop the renovation. Work on the mantras and affirmations. Rustle up the courage to take the tiniest of baby steps to create new habits and new soundtracks. Live with joyful intentions. Realize your life and your very own kingdom purpose. Get out there, and change your world. Keep a list of the words you see yourself becoming on your journey. Put that index card over your RPMs, and just keep saying those words over and again.

Take the journey. You will realize that every baby step forward is worth the struggle and the pain to be free! Go ahead, do the work. Save your life!

Journey

One day, you finally knew
what you had to do, and began,
though the voices around you
kept shouting
their bad advice—
though the whole house began to tremble
and you felt the old tug
at your ankles.
"Mend my life!"
each voice cried.
but you didn't stop.
You knew what you had to do,
though the wind pried
with its stiff fingers
at the very foundations,
though their melancholy
was terrible.

165

It was already late
enough, and a wild night,
and the road full of fallen
branches and stones.
But little by little,
as you left their voice behind,
the stars began to burn
through the sheets of the clouds,
and there was a new voice
which you slowly
recognized as your own,
that kept you company
as you strode deeper and deeper
into the world,
determined to do
the only thing you could do—
determined to save
the only life you could save.

—Mary Oliver[67]

As you see your way out, seeing what's left of those cattails you have pushed through, I would love to hear about your journey out of the swamp of shame. I gladly invite you to contact me through social media at Kingdom Advance Ministry or at kingdomadvanceok@gmail.com.

We hope you will sign up to stay connected to us through our newsletters at https://www.kingdomadvanceministry.com/. Further resources, book updates, and upcoming curriculum workbooks that correlate with this book will all be housed in the Resource section. These curriculum guides could be utilized for camps, small groups, ladies' groups, house groups, personal study, and similar events.

Recommended Books

Anderson, Joan. *A Weekend to Change Your Life: Find Your Authentic Self after a Lifetime of Being All Things to All People*. New York: MJF Books, 2006.

Brown, Brené. *I Thought It Was Just Me (But It Isn't): Making the Journey from "What Will People Think?" to "I Am Enough."* New York, NY: Gotham Books, 2008.

Brown, Brené. *The Gifts of Imperfection: Let Go of Who You Think You're Supposed to Be and Embrace Who You Are*. Center City, Minnesota: Hazelden Publishing, 2010.

Cloud, Dr. Henry. *Changes That Heal*. Grand Rapids, MI: Zondervan, 2018.

Elrod, Hal. *The Miracle Morning: The Not-so-obvious Secret Guaranteed to Transform Your Life (before 8 AM)*. (2012).

Haney, Kim. *Christians and Strongholds: Breaking Free and Staying Free from Internal Captivity.*, 4th ed. Stockton, CA: Women of the Spirit Ministries, 2015.

Hill, Donavon. *I Am3: I Am Who I Am Says I Am*. Tustin CA: Trilogy Christian Publishers, 2020.

Leaf, Dr. Caroline. *Cleaning Up Your Mental Mess*. Grand Rapids, MI: Baker Books, 2021.

Leaf, Dr. Caroline. *Think and Eat Yourself Smart: A Neuroscientific Approach to a Sharper Mind and Healthier Life*. Grand Rapids, MI: Baker Books, 2016.

Martin, Charles. *What If It's True? A Storyteller's Journey with Jesus*. Nashville, TN: W Publishing, 2019.

Niequist, Shauna. *Present Over Perfect: Leaving behind Frantic for a Simpler, More Soulful Way of Living*. Zondervan. 2016

Omartian, Stormie. *Lord, I Want to Be Whole*. Nashville, TN: Thomas Nelson, 2008.

Reimer, Dr. Rob. *Soul Care: Seven Transformational Principles for a Healthy Soul.* Franklin, TN: Carpenter's Son Publishing, 2016.

Van Der Kolk, M.D., Bessel. *The Body Keeps Score: Brain, Mind, and Body in the Healing of Trauma.* New York, NY: Penguin Books, 2014.

Weaver, Joanna. *Having a Mary Heart in a Martha World: Finding Intimacy with God in the Busyness of Life.* Colorado Springs, CO: Waterbrook Press, 2002.

Wiersbe, Warren W. *The Strategy of Satan: How to Detect and Defeat Him.* Tyndale House Publishers, 1979.

Wright, Chester. "Shame: Your Failures Are Not Final," n.d., 83. https://store7336414.company.site/Shame-Seminar-Syllabus-Download-p53302003 https://store7336414.company.site/Syllabus-c13992213 Antioch Store for the syllabus for shame: "Failures are Never Final."

Some of my materials (prayer guides, Scripture note cards, Gospel Bible study, and more) are available for sale on our website:
Kingdom Advance Ministry

Notes

1. Dr. Rob Reimer, *Soul Care: Seven Transformational Principles for a Healthy Soul* (Franklin, TN: Carpenter's Son Publishing, 2016).

2. *Ibid.*

3. Jon Collins, Tim Mackey, BibleProject, Bibleproject.com/explore/video/nephesh-soul/, 2023.

4. *Search for Truth #2* (Hazelwood, MO: Word Aflame Press, 1985), p. 39.

5. *Ibid.*, boldface in original.

6. *Ibid.*

7. *Ibid.*, pp. 39-40.

8. Sonya Matejko, "Don't Just Slow Down Your Schedule, Slow Down Your Soul" (Blog Post: Thought Catalog, 4/17/20).

9. Collins and Mackey, Bibleproject.com/explore/video/judges.

10. Shauna Niequist, *Present over Perfect: Leaving behind Frantic for a Simpler, More Soulful Way of Living* (Grand Rapids, MI: Zondervan, 2016).

11. Dr. James Hughes, Oklahoma Ministers' Retreat, February 2020.

12. Reimer, *Soul Care.*

13. Andy Andrews, *The Traveler's Gift: Seven Decisions That Determine Personal Success* (Thomas Nelson: 2002).

14. Proverbs 26:18-19.

15. Amy Pearson, https://beingamytheblog.com/ and livebrazen.com. At one time the author provided an approval addiction quiz, but the site is not working properly now. It was www.approvalquiz.com.

16. Brené Brown, *The Gifts of Imperfection: Let Go of Who You Think You're Supposed to Be and Embrace Who You Are* (Center City, MN: Hazelden Publishing, 2010).

17. Niequist, *Present over Perfect.*

18. Rev. Jeff Arnold, "The Sovereignty of God: Wise Words 26" (YouTube).

19. Dr. Henry Cloud, *Changes That Heal* (Grand Rapids, MI: Zondervan, 2018).

20. *Ibid.*

21. Reportedly inscribed on the wall of Mother Teresa's children's home in Calcutta, and attributed to her. However, an article in *The New York Times* has since reported (March 8, 2002) that the original version of this poem was written by Kent M. Keith.

22. Niequist, *Present over Perfect.*

23. Reimer, *Soul Care.*

24. Chester Wright, "Shame: Your Failures Are Not Final," (https://store7336414.company.site/Shame-Seminar-Syllabus-Download-p53302003, n.d.) p. 83.

25. American Heritage Dictionary of the English Language.

26. Wright, "Shame."

27. Brown, *The Gifts of Imperfection.*

28. Reimer, *Soul Care.*

29. Wright, "Shame."

30. *Ibid.*, quoting Gershen Kaufman.

31. *Ibid.*

32. *Ibid.*

33. *Ibid.*

34. Brown, *The Gifts of Imperfection.*

35. Reimer, *Soul Care.*

36. Jamie Gilligan, *Violence, Our Deadly Epidemic and Its Causes* (NY: Putnam, 1996).

37. I received assistance with this section from Randa Chance, PLLC, Kainos at kainoscounseling.com.

38. Brown, *The Gifts of Imperfection.*

39. *Ibid.*

40. Hannah Brencher, online course: https://the-writing-intensive.teachable.com/courses/14448 14/lectures/33145367.

41. Dr. Caroline Leaf, *Think and Eat Yourself Smart: A Neuroscientific Approach to a Sharper Mind and Healthier Life* (Grand Rapids, MI: Baker Books, 2016).

42. Reimer, *Soul Care.*

43. https://www.linkedin.com/pulse/lifeand-bamboo-tree-pratik-lahane#:~:text=There's%20a%20famous%20analogy%20of,are%20just%20watering%20the%20dirt.

44. http://www.bamboowisdomacu.com/about/about-bamboo-wisdom/#:~:text=Bamboo%20is%20a%20symbol%20of,it%20resumes%20its%20upright%20position.

45. Leaf, *Think and Eat Yourself Smart.*

46. Wright, "Shame."

47. Warren W. Wiersbe, *The Strategy of Satan: How to Detect and Defeat Him* (Tyndale House Publishers, 1979).

48. Ellen Watson, Kari Herer, and Kate Simpson, *Take Two: A Journal For New Beginnings* (San Franciso, CA: Chronicle Books LLC, 2020).

49. Leaf, *Think and Eat Yourself Smart.*

50. Hal Elrod, *The Miracle Morning: The Not-so-obvious Secret Guaranteed to Transform Your Life (before 8 AM)* (2012).

51. Some of this material about brokenness was taken from a lesson on brokenness from a *Revival By Design* lesson, other parts from material by Nancy Leigh DeMoss.

52. Brencher, the-writing-intensive.

53. Wright, "Shame."

54. *Ibid.*

55. *Ibid.*

56. *Ibid.*

57. Public domain.

58. Matejko, "Don't Just Slow Down Your Schedule."

59. Brown, *Gifts of Imperfection*, pp. 57-61.

60. *Ibid.*, p. 61.

61. Niequist, *Present over Perfect.*

62. Cloud, *Changes That Heal.*

63. *Ibid.*

64. *Ibid.*

65. Elrod, *The Miracle Morning.*

66. Kim Haney, *Christians and Strongholds: Breaking Free and Staying Free from Internal Captivity.*, 4th ed. (Stockton, CA: Women of the Spirit Ministries, 2015).

67. Mary Oliver (Dream Work, Grove/Atlantic, Inc., 1986).

www.ingramcontent.com/pod-product-compliance
Lightning Source LLC
Chambersburg PA
CBHW021145090426
42740CB00008B/942